ADVERTISING
AGENCY
MANAGEMENT

ADVERTISING
AGENCY
MANAGEMENT

Jay McNamara

Dow Jones-Irwin
Homewood, Illinois 60430

© RICHARD D. IRWIN, INC., 1990
Dow Jones-Irwin is a trademark of Dow Jones & Company, Inc.

Sponsoring editor: Susan Glinert Stevens, Ph.D.
Project editor: Jane Lightell
Production manager: Ann Cassady
Jacket designer: Michael S. Finkelman
Compositor: Carlisle Communications, Ltd.
Typeface: 11/13 Century Schoolbook
Printer: Arcata Graphics/Kingsport

Library of Congress Cataloging-in-Publication Data

McNamara, Jay.
    Advertising agency management / Jay McNamara.
      p.   cm.
    ISBN 1-55623-230-6
    1. Advertising agencies—Management. I. Title.
    HF6178.M37   1990
    659.1′125′068—dc20   89–36502
                                                    CIP

Printed in the United States of America
1 2 3 4 5 6 7 8 9 0 K 6 5 4 3 2 1 0 9

For Pat, Mimi, Tony, and Cindy

ACKNOWLEDGMENTS

To Patti Sasson, my assistant; to Susan Glinert, my editor; to Marie Mandry, mentor to many.

FOREWORD

Managing a personal service business—like consulting, law, accounting, or advertising—is different from most other businesses. The *only* asset of these firms is professional talent.

Add the challenge of dealing with creative people who must work together in teams with each other, with other business disciplines, and with a client who is deeply involved in the process, and you begin to understand the skills required to run an advertising agency.

Jay McNamara brings to this book his experience in operating at the top of two world-class agencies. He has worked with the most sophisticated clients in the business, and understands their needs. He has demonstrated an ability not just to manage an agency, but to grow it with current clients and new business.

Anyone who follows the principles in this practical book will find it hard not to succeed. It hits all the big subjects—managing people and client relationships, creating a creative environment and running a good business.

Writing principles is one thing, practicing them is another. This will be a useful reference when things go off the track, as they often do in creative organizations.

Advertising Agency Management will help bring order out of chaos.

July 1989   Kenneth Roman
                                               Chairman
                                               The Ogilvy Group

CONTENTS

INTRODUCTION

There cannot be many careers as exciting as one in advertising. The people in advertising, talented to begin with, represent every possible cultural, ethnic, and geographical background. The teamwork endemic to the business puts these diverse talents together in a pressurized, but mostly rewarding, way.

Because advertisers' end product—the advertising itself—is fundamentally intangible and immeasurable, while at the same time extremely visible, it is constantly the subject of controversy. The enormous amounts of money involved, the high level of competition, and the career stakes for agency and client alike combine to bring out the best and the worst in people.

It is recognized that we live in the information age, and advertising is very much an information medium. The world is moving more and more toward a free market system, and advertising is at the heart of a free market. Technology, particularly satellite transmission, provides more opportunities for consumer communication, brought to the people as always with the economic help of advertising. All these factors bode well for the continued growth of the advertising business.

Advertising, the message, is derived partly by science, partly by art. Advertising strategy, while partly intuitive, is essentially derived from research—numbers that guide the advertiser as to what should be said to whom. The creation and production of the advertising idea is fundamentally a creative endeavor. The strategy and the idea are science and art working together toward a business end.

As with the advertising itself, the management of an advertising agency is part science and part art. Because of the people nature of the business, the art of dealing with people— motivating them and managing them—is at the very heart of the management issue. Yet, there are a number of proven techniques, processes, and rules (science) that are part of the advertising management task.

This book sets down thoughts, rules, processes, and guidelines to aid the agency manager in the day-to-day operation of an advertising agency. Whether someone is an established agency manager, an aspiring manager, or a student contemplating the agency business, this book is intended to help in dealing with the spectrum of agency management issues.

CHAPTER 1

AGENCY POSITIONING

As participants in the marketing process, advertising agencies are asked to contribute to their clients' marketing, to help develop marketing plans and programs, and to formulate advertising strategy. Specifically, agencies are in the business of assisting their clients in the positioning of their brands in the marketplace. Correctly identifying the proper positioning for a brand is an essential part of marketing.

Positioning a brand means establishing it as something unique and desirable in its particular category—as something that offers its users some clearly defined benefits, both tangible and intangible. Positioning helps distinguish the brand from its competition, thereby making the brand more attractive to its users, as well as to its potential users.

Yet, even though agencies help clients in the positioning of their brands, few agencies spend much time thinking about positioning themselves in the marketplace. The implications of this failing are broad. If an agency has not carefully thought through its positioning, then it will not present a clear identity to its critical audiences: its clients and prospective clients and its employees, both current and future. Clients and prospective clients, employees and prospective employees are faced with an array of choices among advertising agencies. Any agency that has not analyzed the competitive marketplace to determine its unique place within it risks becoming lost in the maze of choice.

ELEMENTS OF POSITIONING

What are the elements of choice with regard to defining a positioning for an advertising agency? For what does the agency want to stand? Obviously, an ongoing agency's existing situation will have a controlling effect on its positioning. Nevertheless, it is what the agency's ideal positioning should be—to what it should aspire in the future—that makes the positioning process critical.

There are a number of agencies that have been successful in positioning themselves in the marketplace. Among the big agencies, Grey has succeeded in establishing a reputation as a strong, strategically helpful packaged goods agency and has prospered in the process. Young & Rubicam, BBDO, and Ogilvy & Mather have established reputations for delivering strong marketing thinking combined with effective creativity. In recent years, Leo Burnett has established a strong positioning and reputation for developing successful selling ideas, as has J. Walter Thompson. Among the medium-sized agencies, Hill, Holliday has developed an excellent creative reputation in the last five years, as have Chiat Day and Hal Riney. None of these positive reputations have come about casually. In each case, much effort has been devoted to achieving the desired positive positioning.

The process for arriving at a desired positioning can be utilized by an agency of any size. This process is based primarily on answering a series of fundamental questions.

The first question is, What kinds of communication services should the agency offer? The answer to this critical question will determine the kinds of clients for whom the agency is best suited, the type of talent the agency will need to perform its services, and the fees the agency should charge for its services. In a consumer agency, which is the central subject of this book, there is an array of service possibilities to offer clients. The complete communication agency would offer, in addition to basic advertising services (such as research, media, creative, and account management), direct marketing, sales promotion, public relations, yellow pages, design, and, perhaps, health-care expertise. To be well-situated in the future, it behooves agencies to look for services, such as those, to increase the total number of services offered. More and more clients in the future will look for agencies that can provide a totally integrated communication program.

An example of an integrated agency communication program is the client using consumer advertising (TV and print), plus a direct-mail program, plus sales promotion services, provided by one agency. Another example is the client utilizing consumer advertising and public relations services from the same agency. The agency objective is to ensure that the communication to the consumer is synchronized, supportive, and integrated to the point where the total communication impact becomes greater than the sum of the individual communication efforts. The advertising industry has a long way to go in achieving this desired integration, however, and currently not many clients believe they are receiving a successful combination of communication efforts from their agencies. Nevertheless, the clients' needs and the advertisers' desires are there, and most agencies are making efforts to accommodate these needs. In March of 1989, Ogilvy & Mather announced a management realignment aimed at providing clients with better total communication programs. A new class of senior executives, trained in a variety of communication disciplines, will provide clients with objective advice on the best means of solving marketing problems. A later section in this book deals with the barriers to successful integration and discusses how integrated agency communication can be achieved.

A second fundamental question is, To what kinds of clients does the agency want to appeal? The answer to this question will partly derive from the existing client list, partly from the range of services the agency has determined to offer, and partly on a projection of future clients. For example, if the existing client base is mostly in the packaged goods market, the agency may be forced to position itself as the ideal packaged goods agency, making sure that it can properly service packaged goods clients. However, the world comprises a variety of client types, such as fashion, entertainment, retail, service, financial, office equipment, and publishing. Each of these industries has unique communication needs. An agency that determines that it wants to appeal to any given one will have to craft itself accordingly.

For example, if an agency wishes to attract retail accounts (and certainly most agencies do), then it must demonstrate to a prospect that it has the capability to develop advertising that will make the cash register ring, that it can deliver this kind of communication on a continuous, day-in, day-out basis, and that it can provide this service on a very affordable basis. Because retailers are acutely sensitive to costs and because they are constantly changing their messages, these messages must be produced at very low unit costs.

In complete contrast to the preceding example is the agency that wishes to attract a consumer account where the product's appeal is basically emotional, such as that of a soft drink. Here, the agency must be able to develop powerful selling ideas that emotionally move consumers. Particularly in TV, the ability to produce advertising that is bigger than life, musically strong, and generally of the highest order in terms of production values is absolutely essential. Since the advertising for this type of product will run over sustained periods of time, the cost of making the messages is less of a concern for this client than it is for the retailer whose messages must be constantly altering.

Considering these two contrasting examples, it can be seen that a single given agency, unless it is quite large, is unlikely to combine the right talent and experience, not to mention the overall agency mentality, to achieve a successful positioning that includes both retail accounts *and* packaged goods, such as soft drinks. Therefore, answering the question as to the kinds of clients an agency wishes to attract has serious repercussions.

Over and above its service capabilities and the nature of its client list, an agency must determine which of its functional abilities it wants to include in its central positioning. The alternatives include such basic functions as creative, research, media, account management, and strategic planning, as well as the range of service specialties noted previously, including direct mail, sales promotion, and yellow pages. The truth is, only a few of the giant agencies can even hope to position themselves as all things to all people. Smaller agencies and, importantly, regional branches of mega-agencies must make directed positioning decisions. If an agency decides that it will be positioned first and foremost as a creative resource, agency efforts to make this positioning a reality necessarily leave few resources for other functions. Similarly, if an agency decides to position itself in its market as the most adroit in strategic planning, then its emphasis on other disciplines is diminished.

Another aspect of positioning an agency must consider is the geographical range it wishes to claim. Unless the agency is already part of a worldwide network, this question can be challenging. To what distance is the agency willing to go to capture an account, recognizing the greater the distance, the greater the competition and the greater the implications on services and staffing? If an agency is located in North Carolina, for example, and over the years has developed a strong reputation with financial services clients, it should think twice about seeking as a client a bank located in Atlanta. While Atlanta might only be an hour's plane ride away, the day-to-day nature of a bank's communication needs could be so demanding that the agency would lose money on the account. If the agency is seeking to position itself as a Southeastern regional agency, however, then an opportunity to gain a foothold in Atlanta might override cost considerations.

The desire to expand geographically is enticing, but many agencies have learned to their dismay that overreaching geographically can be enormously draining, financially and otherwise. Any geographical expansion must be considered carefully. Unfortunately, much expansion occurs as the result of a client call from out of town, and before it knows it, an agency has some business in another city. This is business by reaction, not growth as a result of carefully planned positioning.

The history and culture of an agency play an important and sometimes controlling part in determining positioning. Who the founders were, for what the founders stood, who the early and current clients were and are, for what, if anything, the agency is now known, what victories (or defeats) the agency has suffered in the marketplace, who the current principals are and for what they are known, and a myriad of cultural aspects, such as physical location and work environment, work style, and morale, are all factors to consider in developing the agency's positioning. For example, if an agency was founded by three people who were known for their packaged goods expertise, the agency's accounts, including its two largest, are mostly packaged goods and the whole mentality and capability of the agency is oriented toward packaged goods brands, it is not a good idea to pretend that the agency is well-suited for an airline account or an entertainment company. The required communication needs of these other accounts are quite different from those of packaged goods companies.

How the agency ultimately defines its positioning will have a major effect on how it prices its services. The range of services offered, the kinds of clients served, the geographical scope of the agency, the agency's known areas of strength, and its overall reputation will have an effect on pricing. This subject is dealt with in specific terms in Chapter 9.

CURRENT PERCEPTIONS OF THE AGENCY

Unless the agency is one of the very largest as researched every few years by a U.S. Harris poll, it will not have a clear understanding of how it is perceived in the marketplace. Even local branches of giant agencies will have reputations that differ from the parent agency. Therefore, as part of the positioning process, it behooves all agencies to clearly understand what they are.

How can an agency develop a positioning that will take it into the future if it does not have a fix on what type of agency it is today? An excellent and affordable means for making a current assessment is an employee survey. An employee survey not only can provide valuable insight into the agency's current state, but it also can act as a benchmark for future studies aimed at defining trends on a variety of dimensions.

A prototypical memo to employees and a questionnaire are shown in Exhibit 1–1. The questionnaire should be given to all employees and should be coded by function, not by individual name, so that people will feel free to comment without fear of recrimination.

EXHIBIT 1–1
Prototypical Staff Memo to All Employees

Your management is in the process of evaluating our agency from many standpoints in order to better assess our current position in the marketplace, as well as to aid us in the development of a business plan that will help us grow in the future.

As a member of the agency, each of you will be a participant in that growth; each of you has a stake in that future; and each of you has an opinion about our agency and about our competition. Therefore, we are seeking your help in gaining a better understanding of the agency as it exists today.

We would like each of you to answer the questions attached to this memo and to return the questionnaire by Friday. Importantly, you do not need to identify yourself, only your department; your answers will remain completely confidential. When the answers have all been analyzed, we will hold a meeting to share with you the combined opinions of all employees. Similarly, when we have completed our business plan, we will present that to you so that we all know the course we have set for ourselves.

A series of questions appear on the following pages. Please answer all the questions, giving the most candid answers possible. We are trying to get as clear a perception of ourselves and our competition as possible. If you have any questions, please call_____in the research department.

1. Shown below are the important agencies in our market. Indicate your familiarity with each agency.

Agency	Familiarity			
	Very	Somewhat	Not Very	Not at all
A	4	3	2	1
B	4	3	2	1
C	4	3	2	1
D	4	3	2	1
E	4	3	2	1
F	4	3	2	1
G	4	3	2	1
H	4	3	2	1
I	4	3	2	1
J	4	3	2	1

EXHIBIT 1-1
(continued)

2. Below are a series of characteristics often used to describe advertising agencies. For each, indicate what you believe best describes the importance of that characteristic when evaluating an agency.

Characteristic	Degree of Importance			
	Essential	*Very*	*Not Very*	*Not at All*
Creative ability	4	3	2	1
Strategic direction	4	3	2	1
Account management	4	3	2	1
Financial accountability	4	3	2	1
Involvement in client's business	4	3	2	1
Global network	4	3	2	1
Research capabilities	4	3	2	1
Direct marketing capabilities	4	3	2	1
Sales promotion capabilities	4	3	2	1
Public relations capabilities	4	3	2	1

3. Please rate our own agency on these same characteristics, using the rating scale shown.

Characteristic	Rating			
	Excellent	*Good*	*Average*	*Poor*
Creative ability	4	3	2	1
Strategic direction	4	3	2	1
Account management	4	3	2	1
Financial accountability	4	3	2	1
Involvement in client's business	4	3	2	1
Global network	4	3	2	1
Research capabilities	4	3	2	1
Direct marketing capabilities	4	3	2	1
Sales promotion capabilities	4	3	2	1
Public relations capabilities	4	3	2	1

4. In the boxes shown below, for each agency make a mark (x) if you think a characteristic accurately describes the agency. Make as many marks as you believe are fitting for each agency. If you do not know about an agency, mark the last box, "Don't Know."

Agency	Creative	Hot	Stodgy	Strategic	Arrogant	Professional	Innovative	Responsive	Fun	Intelligent	Profitable	Don't Know
A												
B												
C												
D												
E												
F												
G												
H												
I												
J												

EXHIBIT 1-1
(continued)

5. Rank our own agency on these same characteristics.

Characteristic	Describes Us			
	Completely	*A Lot*	*Somewhat*	*Not at All*
Creative	4	3	2	1
Hot	4	3	2	1
Stodgy	4	3	2	1
Strategic	4	3	2	1
Arrogant	4	3	2	1
Professional	4	3	2	1
Innovative	4	3	2	1
Responsive	4	3	2	1
Fun	4	3	2	1
Intelligent	4	3	2	1
Profitable	4	3	2	1

6. Listed below are the departments in our agency. For each, provide your opinion of the department.

Department	Rating			
	Excellent	*Good*	*Average*	*Poor*
Creative	4	3	2	1
Account management	4	3	2	1
Research	4	3	2	1
Media	4	3	2	1
Traffic	4	3	2	1
Accounting	4	3	2	1
Billing	4	3	2	1
Direct marketing	4	3	2	1
Sales promotion	4	3	2	1
Public relations	4	3	2	1
Strategic planning	4	3	2	1
Personnel	4	3	2	1
Top management	4	3	2	1

EXHIBIT 1-1
(concluded)

7. To help us analyze the answers to the questionnaire, please fill in the answers to the following questions. Remember, this is a confidential process. We do not need to know your name.

Sex_____
Age_____
Years in the advertising business_____
Years with our agency_____
Department_____
Title_____

Lastly, please tell us your opinion of what should be done to improve the agency and what specifically should be done to allow you to do your job better.

FOLLOW-UP TO QUESTIONNAIRE

It is critical that the results of the questionnaire analysis are shared with all employees in an agencywide meeting. Otherwise, credibility is lost and it is likely that employees will suspect management has secretly analyzed the questionnaire and soon will be taking action without informing the employees. The result of this secrecy will be rampant speculation and rumormongoring by the employees as to what is in store for the agency and for them, in particular. This will have the opposite effect of that intended by the whole positioning process, which is to have an informed, unified agency staff marching toward common goals.

The questionnaire is part of the assessment process management uses to determine the agency's proper positioning and, as is shown in the next chapter, to develop a solid business plan. All employees should be brought into this process so that they can feel a part of it. Indeed, if properly used, employees do in time become a part of the process. Over a period of years, as subsequent business plans are developed, additional employee surveys should be made so that employee perceptions of the agency are tracked. As the agency succeeds in meeting its objectives, everyone can feel he or she has played a role in the success.

OTHER SOURCES FOR AGENCY ASSESSMENT

While employee opinions of the agency are the primary gauge of an agency's standing, there are other sources of marketplace assessment. One such source is client evaluations. If some clients have not evaluated the agency recently, it behooves agency management to urge those clients to do so. An examination of all of an agency's client evaluations will provide a good perspective on the strengths and weaknesses of the agency and will aid in the self-evaluation process.

Another excellent source of assessment is media personalities. The media are in constant contact with a spectrum of agencies. As a result, many media people have a feel for the agencies with which they deal and are able to comment intelligently on strengths and weaknesses of and differences between agencies. The media also deal directly with clients and are therefore often aware of client opinions and perceptions of their advertising agencies. A careful gathering of media information will help an agency in its self-assessment process.

Self-assessment—determining what the agency's position is today and, more importantly, what its marketing positioning should be tomorrow—is central to the business planning process. This process is intended to provide an agency with a business plan—a clear blueprint for action to help the agency achieve its goals.

MISSION STATEMENT

At an early stage in the planning process, every agency should write a mission statement—a one-page, succinct statement about what the agency stands and a document that can be proudly displayed throughout the agency—so that everyone will know the agency's essential purpose. The mission statement is created when management has arrived at the agency's position. It should be formulated in conjunction with the business planning process, the subject of the next chapter. Since the mission statement becomes the agency's credo, it must honestly reflect the agency's purpose, people, culture, and aspirations.

As with anything creative, a good deal of soul-searching and strategic analysis must occur before an actual mission statement can be written. Only after management has carefully thought through the essential elements of the agency's mission can the actual statement be written. Obviously, since the mission statement will become a lasting document intended to inspire all current and future employees, it must be written in a clear, concise, and compelling manner. An example of a mission statement is shown in Exhibit 1–2.

Once an agency has clearly faced the positioning issues, both present and future, and has been able to write a succinct mission statement, it is ready to begin the business planning process. This is the subject of the next chapter.

EXHIBIT 1–2
Hypothetical Mission Statement

Our agency is known to be young, vibrant, energetic, and, most of all, creative. We have the reputation of being the most creative agency in our market. Everything we do should center around our creativity.

We recognize that our fundamental purpose is to create ideas to further our clients' businesses.

We must be careful to do business only with companies that respect creativity, that are willing to be open and honest business partners, and that will compensate us profitably.

In keeping with our reputation for award-winning advertising, we will continue to enter such competitions and will reward the agency individuals responsible for the award-winning efforts.

In order to control our growth and maintain our focus on creativity, we will confine ourselves to one central office facility for the foreseeable future.

Our surrounding physical environment must reflect our vigor and creativity. Our planned new suburban office, complete with eating and athletic facilities, should reflect in every way our creative focus.

Basically, we believe that if we concentrate on the goal of being the most creative agency, we will continue to attract the best talent and, as a result, will be profitable as well. We will also have a lot of fun in the process.

CHAPTER 2

━━━━━━

BUSINESS PLANNING

A good business plan can noticeably improve an advertising agency's operation. This chapter deals with the purpose of the business plan, the responsibility for completing and monitoring the business plan, individual components of the plan, and how to write a business plan, as well as issues relating to timing and follow-up. This planning process is useful for both small agencies ($20 to 25 million in billings) and those with larger billings.

PURPOSE OF THE BUSINESS PLAN

The purpose of the business plan is to provide a clear set of objectives and strategies for agency management. The plan will enable management to move the agency from its current state to a more advanced one in the future. Since the plan is put together by the top operatives of the agency, it is an opportunity for these people to meet and candidly assess the status of the agency and to establish where they believe the agency should be in several years. The business plan should become a living document, something to which the operational management can refer on an ongoing basis to assess the progress they are making in achieving the established goals. The business plan can be completed for an individual operating unit—for example, an office in a given city—or it can be completed for a larger organization, such as a regional group consisting of a variety of agencies from different disciplines and locations. The plan can even be used by an agency to develop a worldwide plan. On a more limited scope, a plan can be developed for a function, such as account management, within an individual unit of an advertising agency.

RESPONSIBILITY

It is the responsibility of the unit's key operating executives to develop a business plan, with the senior executive present having ultimate responsibility. For example, in an individual agency office, the key operating members include the head of the office, as well as the directors of the various functions, such as account management, creative, media, and research, and key individuals from finance and administration. Depending on the situation, several other key individuals within the unit may be present, perhaps those largely responsible for either account handling or creative assignments. The ideal number of people attending such a session is 8 to 10, although it is possible to conduct an effective session with as many as a dozen people involved.

It is essential that the planning meeting is held at an off-campus site so interruptions are kept to a minimum. Because of the nature of the subject matter and the atmosphere desired, the more remote the location, the better the results. A minimum of two full days is required to put together the elements of the business plan.

THE MODERATOR

One person must moderate and orchestrate the development of a business plan. The person capable of accomplishing this is unique—very few people in the advertising industry have the required skills and experience to be effective in this role. Ideally, the individual who moderates the group is from outside the organization altogether, that is, someone who can be looked upon as totally objective in the role. Obviously, the individual from an agency's senior management who is conducting a business planning session for an agency subunit must be respected by the entire organization. Otherwise, the individual might be viewed as a management spy and the people might not be as candid and productive as they would be if they trusted the moderator. It is the role of the moderator to establish and maintain an open, friendly, and collaborative attitude for the business planning session. Someone who is skilled in strategic planning, but who also has real advertising agency management experience, is ideal for this position.

PREPARING FOR THE MEETING

Prior to assembling the entire group, the moderator must meet one-on-one at least once with the individuals who will attend the planning session. This will give the moderator a sense of how each assesses the agency's current situation and its future and, importantly, what these individuals believe the agency's key problems are. After meeting with each participant (hopefully on several occasions) and analyzing this feedback, the moderator can effectively lead the group since she or he will have a good sense of the overall state of the agency.

ELEMENTS OF THE BUSINESS PLAN

A finished business plan will have a one- to two-page statement of the current condition of the agency, a similar-length statement of the desired agency three years hence, and a set of objectives and strategies for bridging the gap between the two. Accordingly, a full day's work must be devoted to arriving at an honest assessment of the agency's current condition, as well as a parallel statement of the desired agency three years hence. The initial session should deal with the external and internal elements currently affecting the business. All factors, big and small, should be considered during this discussion. These factors, such as competition, the economy, the government, environmental factors, and the media, should be discussed in detail. This discussion will establish a background and context for creating a statement of the agency's current position, a "statement of today."

STATEMENT OF TODAY

The statement of today should comprise a variety of elements descriptive of the agency as of the current point in time. These elements include agency size (absolute and relative), client base (type of clients, size, relationship, growth potential, and national versus local), agency product (objective analysis of the quality of the agency's product in absolute terms and also versus competition, awards status, quality of product by medium), people (quality and quantity at all levels and within all functions), profits (income, expenses, trends, all in absolute and in terms of competition), competitive framework (detailed understanding of the agency's competition), administrative, legal, and financial resource evaluation, real estate situation (space needs, costs, moving costs), and environmental and cultural aspects.

These are the key elements in describing an advertising agency. It is important that the group is as candid and as open as possible in describing the current condition of the agency according to these elements. This requires a good deal of soul-searching and honesty on the part of the group, as well as an ability to be open with each other. If the business plan is to be meaningful, it is essential that the statement of today is an accurate reflection of the agency's true condition. An example of a statement of today and a complete prototypical plan are shown in Exhibit 2–1.

STATEMENT OF TOMORROW

The statement of tomorrow is a snapshot of what the agency management wants the agency to become in three years. Each of the aspects described in the statement of today should also be described in the statement of tomorrow, but obviously at higher levels. The statement of tomorrow should be one that is ambitious, but realistically obtainable. If not, it can become a frustrating and demoralizing document for the management as over time it begins to realize that it cannot obtain its envisioned goal.

As stated, the group formulating the statement of today and the statement of tomorrow should spend a full day working on

EXHIBIT 2–1
Statement of Today

We are a $75 million, full-service agency, third largest in size in our geographical market. We see ourselves and are perceived by others as an agency with strong account management and strategic skills, good media and research capabilities, but with only average creative abilities.

Our clients are mostly packaged goods companies. We are dominated by our largest account, which represents 50 percent of our income and 65 percent of our profits. While the agency is of average profitability relative to industry norms, this is due to the income derived from our largest account; our smaller clients are mostly unprofitable.

Our staff is loyal, home grown, and long in tenure, which on the one hand makes internal communications and the work process smooth (since we know each other well), but on the other hand makes us stodgy and a bit too comfortable. We have very few lower- and middle-level people of star quality.

Our training programs, particularly in account management, media, and research are extensive and have proven over time to be effective. This is not so in the creative area, where very little training has taken place in recent years.

Agency growth in recent years has been slow and mostly from our existing client base. Our new business record is poor, and of late we have not reached the finals of most of the agency competitions in which we have participated.

Our internal communications are good and most people have a sense of what the agency is doing. Morale is fair; it has been lowered by our lack of new business success. We have been remiss about external communications since the departure of our public relations executive last year.

We have little expertise in the communication skills related to consumer advertising, such as direct marketing, public relations, sales promotion, and the yellow pages. As a result, we are vulnerable to fuller service agencies and have had to turn away client business because of this lack of expertise.

Overall, we are a successful, reasonably sized agency recognized for our strong account management. We do, however, lack the creative spark and reputation needed for greater growth from old and from potential clients.

---

the plans. Once these two statements have been developed, it is time for the group to turn to the important task of setting the objectives and strategies that will move the agency to the desired goal. A sample statement of tomorrow is shown in Exhibit 2–2.

EXHIBIT 2–2
Statement of Tomorrow

In the three years since we created our statement of today, we have grown into a $115 million agency due to three consecutive 15 percent growth years. As a result, we have achieved a ranking of second largest agency in our geographical area and are closing in on the number one agency.

Our growth has come mostly (two-thirds) from several new business accounts. Moreover, our new clients are representative of the service sector of the economy.

Partly because of our success and also due to an extensive recruitment program, we have attracted to our organization a number of young individuals of star quality.

Our agency is better recognized both inside and out as being creative. This is the result of our new business success, of our being the recipient of several creative awards, and of the hiring of a new public relations director who has successfully publicized the agency's creative product.

We have extended our training program curriculum, particularly in the creative area, and have mandated that all employees participate in at least two training programs per year. These training programs are aimed at improving employees' professional skills.

Our profitability levels have improved dramatically; our income growth has exceeded our expense increases, thereby improving our margins. We have made fair, but profitable, compensation agreements with our new clients and with several of our old clients (which have benefited from our efforts and success). Accordingly, we are much less dependent on our largest account, both from a revenue and a profitability standpoint.

We are closer to the ideal of being a total communications agency since adding expertise in direct marketing, sales promotion, and public relations.

Overall, we are looked upon as being the hottest creative agency in our area. We are contacted frequently by younger talent and by prospective clients as they seek an agency of choice.

BUSINESS PLAN OBJECTIVES AND STRATEGIES

The effective business plan should contain no more than five or six objectives, each with a set of strategies geared towards accomplishing the objective. It is essential that the wording in these objectives and strategies is as specific as possible, that the desired actions are measurable, that due dates have been set for the desired actions, and that individuals are made responsible for achieving the objectives by implementing the strategies. An example of objectives and strategies is shown in Exhibit 2–3.

EXHIBIT 2–3
Agency Objectives and Strategies

Objective A: Creative

Our highest priority is to improve the agency's creative product. This will result
in increased billings from both current and new clients, an improved ability
to attract and keep better people, and an overall sense of being an agency
that is at the leading edge of its business.

Strategies	Responsibility	Due Date
1. Increase the payroll budget of the creative department by 10 percent.	General manager	Immediately
2. Create an extra $25 thousand bonus pool to quickly reward people who generate ideas. Publicize these special awards.	General manager	Immediately
3. Hire an additional young "star" writer/art director team.	Creative director	Within four months
4. Develop a comprehensive basic training program for creative people. Involve everyone.	Creative director with operations committee	Within six months
5. Participate in all important industry creative awards competitions.	Creative director	Immediately
6. Celebrate creative "victories."	Creative director	As they occur
7. Hold an agencywide meeting announcing new emphasis on creativity.	General manager	Within one month

Objective B: Financial

Develop a financial plan that is consistent with the agency's overall goals,
including profits.

Strategies	Responsibility	Due Date
1. Analyze individual accounts according to profitability.	Financial manager	Immediately

EXHIBIT 2-3
(continued)

Strategies	Responsibility	Due Date
2. Develop a plan for dealing with clients that are not profitable to the agency. Implement plan by talking to clients.	Operations committee	Within two months
3. Develop a new profit plan that provides for a 15 percent increase in revenues and profits in year 1.	General manager with operations committee	Within one month
4. Develop a new expense plan (within the agreed profit plan) that permits a 10 percent increase in compensation to the creative department.	General manager with operations committee	Within two months

Objective C: New Business

Develop a new business plan and program aimed at achieving the agency's new business goals.

Strategies	Responsibility	Due Date
1. Establish a new business task force.	General manager	Immediately
2. Identify key prospects.	General manager with new business task force	Within one month
3. Develop plan of attack to attract prospects, including possible house advertising, mailings, and contacts with key prospect executives.	General manager with new business task force	Within two months
4. Develop and implement presentation skills course for all key executives.	General manager	Within one month

EXHIBIT 2-3 (*continued*)

Strategies	Responsibility	Due Date
5. Develop a plan for gaining and utilizing information about prospects.	Media director	Within one month
6. Develop a plan for involving key executives in important industry associations and functions. Look for speech opportunities.	General manager	Immediately

Objective D: Human Resources

Develop and implement a human resources program consistent with agency's overall goals. Specifically, this program will attract younger people, reward key personnel, and advance training, especially in the creative area.

Strategies	Responsibility	Due Date
1. Identify the top 20 young advertising individuals in the market. Meet with each, with the goal of hiring six to be part of the future management.	Operations Committee	Within one month
2. Develop a plan and provide a fund for immediately rewarding individuals for creative excellence.	General manager with operations committee	Within one month
3. Appoint an agencywide training director to enhance and supervise all training and, importantly, to develop a training program for the creative department.	Operations committee	Immediately
4. Hire a new director of public relations.	General manager	As soon as possible

EXHIBIT 2-3 (*concluded*)

Strategies	*Responsibility*	*Due Date*
5. Appoint a new technology director who will be responsible for developing a plan to utilize new technologies throughout the agency.	Operations committee	Within one month
6. Make sure each and every employee is evaluated once a year. Review and update evaluation forms.	Department heads	Within six months

Objective E: Special Expertise

Develop a plan for hiring or acquiring resources in allied agency fields.

Strategies	*Responsibility*	*Due Date*
1. Analyze each client to determine degree to which each uses or could use the following expertise: sales promotion, yellow pages, medical, direct marketing, public relations.	Individual account directors	As soon as possible
2. Based on this assessment, prioritize areas of desired expertise.	Operations committee	Within one month
3. Determine alternatives for obtaining desired expertise, either through hiring of specific individuals or through acquisition.	General manager	Within two months
4. Approach selected individuals and/or acquisition candidates.	General manager	Within three months

The process by which the group determines the key objectives is an outgrowth of the earlier discussions about the
external and internal factors affecting the agency, as well as the
statements of today and tomorrow. A consensus should determine the key objectives that will lead the agency to its improvement goals. Success is a powerful motivator; therefore, the
objectives and strategies should be assigned completion dates of
no longer than 12 months from implementation, even though
the overall plan has a three-year perspective. Since the business
plan is intended to be a living, working document, it should be
updated annually. This necessarily results in another three-year
projection of the picture of the agency, as well as objectives and
strategies that have a shorter completion cycle.

RESULTS OF THE BUSINESS
PLANNING MEETING

An effective planning meeting can be an exhilarating experience for an agency management group. If they have not been-
talking to each other in these terms heretofore, the meeting can
be a true catharsis. The very idea of the top 8 to 12 individuals
in an agency going off for several days to discuss the true issues
facing them, honestly assessing the agency's current condition
and its future, and the work involved in setting solid objectives
and strategies can only result in a more cohesive and enthusiastic management team.

Following the planning sessions, it is the role of the senior
manager or head of the office to ensure that periodic meetings are
held to update the group on progress in meeting the various
objectives and strategies. If not, like any plan, the business plan
will merely gather dust and be of no long-term benefit whatsoever.
Agencies that make the planning process part of the day-to-day
management scheme are those that will prosper as a result.

FOLLOW-UP

Once completed, a business plan should be shared with the
entire agency. Assuming all employees helped the agency in the

self-assessment of marketplace position, it is essential that all agency people are provided the details of the business plan. The object here is to allow them to be participants in the agency's dream, to know and to share the agency's hopes for itself.

Equally important is the need to monitor the business plan, to make it a living document. Quarterly assessment of progress toward meeting due dates is essential. An effective business plan, as noted, is actionable, measurable, and has clearly defined responsibilities and due dates.

Finally, the business planning process is never ending. Each year a new assessment of the agency's state of being must be made, and a new three-year plan must be developed. As the agency achieves success in meeting some of its goals, enthusiasm for even greater aspirations will be generated, and the entire agency will feel a sense of shared success.

CHAPTER 3

AGENCY ORGANIZATION

While the agency business is not complicated, many agencies complicate their businesses simply because they are not organized properly. A variety of operational pitfalls should be avoided so that neither employees nor clients are confused as to just how the agency operates. Clients, who are by definition businesspeople, judge agencies in part on how they conduct their own business. Organizational problems can be visible symbols of agency mismanagement.

This chapter discusses the organizational problems and pitfalls inherent to the agency business. It also points out proven ways to achieve a better run agency through intelligent organizational planning and practice.

THE PYRAMID

Like most companies, agencies are organized in the shape of a pyramid, with the chief executive officer (CEO) at the pinnacle and the rest of the organization flowing down from that point. What is often forgotten is that within this flow, lines of organization and reporting must be absolutely clear to everyone, both inside and outside the agency. Any fuzziness in reporting lines confuses everyone and helps breed politics, the enemy of good agency management.

For example, if some senior account management people report directly to the office head, while others report to a director of client services, who then reports to the office head, the latter group become second-class citizens since they do not have the same direct access to the top. An astute client observing such a situation would insist that the person assigned to that client's account report directly to the office head. Clients want to be able to access the best resources of the agency and, accordingly, want people who can make things happen within the agency assigned to their businesses.

ORGANIZING AT THE TOP

An agency needs two committees for the proper conduct of its business: an operations committee and an executive committee. The operations committee or group is concerned with the day-to-day operations of the agency. This committee should comprise the CEO, the chief operating officer (COO) or president, and those individuals who are clearly responsible for the workings of the company. In a worldwide agency, this would include the area or regional directors, the most senior managers of multinational accounts, plus the senior executives for finance, creative, media, and research. In other words, the people responsible for the agency's product, for client relationships with its biggest accounts, and for the day-to-day operations and finances of the agency would be members of the operations committee.

In an individual agency unit or office, the operations committee, in addition to the CEO and COO, includes the department heads, including finance, plus two or three of the most senior account management individuals. An optional member of the operations committee is the person responsible for new business development, although most likely this responsibility belongs to a very senior agency officer who is already a member of the committee.

In addition to day-to-day operations, the operations committee also creates and monitors the business plan, as discussed in Chapter 2. Because of these major responsibilities, the operations committee must meet regularly, no less than every two weeks.

The second management committee, called the executive or policy committee, concerns itself with policy issues affecting the agency, such as legal, personnel, and public relations. The committee should consist of the CEO, the heads of the departments concerned with policy (certainly those functions noted before), plus the chief financial officer (CFO).

Because of the nature of the subject matter, the policy committee need not meet as often as the operations committee. Once a month or even quarterly is sufficient.

Only three individuals—the CEO, the COO, and the CFO—serve on both the operations committee and the policy committee.

LINE VERSUS STAFF

In terms of line versus staff individuals, agencies must constantly be wary of the tendency of all agency organizations to increase the staff as opposed to the organization's line. Line people are those account management, creative, media, and research people directly involved in making the advertising and selling it to the agency's clients. Staff people are not directly involved with the agency's product or clients. Rather, they fill the administrative, financial, legal, personnel, and/or or marketing positions. All clerical employees are also considered staff. Since the line people must do the work—create it and sell it to the clients—they must receive the bulk of the rewards of the business.

Too often, line people who have moved along in their careers are put into staff jobs just to keep them happy and within the company. Existing staff individuals tend to insist upon additional staff people to help them. Because of these two conditions, before long the agency is outweighed by staff. When this happens, the agency can become overly internalized and political, concerned with matters that are not relevant to clients. An annual zero-based organizational analysis is required to ensure that the size of the staff does not get out of hand. As with zero-based budgeting, zero-based organizational planning starts with a blank page and works toward developing the ideal organization based on need. Such a system requires each element in the organization to rejustify from time to time its reason for being.

Line people in an agency are very sensitive to the staff and by and large resent their power and presence, particularly if it is known that the staff has very little to do with the agency's product or clients. An office head or president who is surrounded by staff can often be misled by these staff individuals. This creates a major problem. The only truth that exists in an advertising agency operation is what the client thinks is true. If the client thinks the agency is underperforming despite all evidence to the contrary, then the agency *is* underperforming. Therefore, anything that tends to blur this reality (which staff people often do) tends to lead the agency away from the truth.

A staff individual, as an example, might recommend reducing the number of people on a given account to reduce costs and to increase profits. If the senior management of the agency is not cognizant of the ramifications of such an action on that account, disaster could lie ahead in terms of reduced agency output on the account and of client dissatisfaction.

OVERALL MANAGEMENT ORGANIZATIONAL ATTITUDE

It is the manager's job to make sure that a great deal of flexibility exists within an agency, that a spirit of teamwork is present, that barriers to interaction among product groups and between departments are reduced, and that all of this leads to a high level of efficiency, while maintaining quality in the agency's product. To do this, the head of the agency must be present and involved in day-to-day activities, obviously interested in the product, and very close to the agency's clients. As was said earlier, the only truth resides in clients.

TASK FORCES

From time to time, the CEO and the operations committee should utilize task forces to analyze agency issues and to make suitable recommendations. In its periodic meetings, the operations committee can easily identify problem areas that need attention. The use of a task force made up of half a dozen or so people representing different agency functions to analyze a problem and to provide a recommendation for resolution is a good way to get quick answers and to build morale. The day-to-day working people in an agency are most aware of existing problems, but too often they are not asked to provide opinions on and solutions to these problems. A good agency operation at any given time should have three or four task forces at work on identified issues. It is critical that whatever recommendations are made by these small groups are acted upon in a forthright and visible manner so that everyone feels that the effort was worthwhile. Accordingly, task forces should have a short existence, certainly no longer than one year in duration.

TITLES

Agency titles should clearly indicate the roles and responsibilities of agency personnel. This rule of management, however, is violated on a regular basis. Agency management becomes trapped by what it sees as the need to "promote" individuals within the agency for a variety of reasons. One such reason is that an individual is no longer suitable for his or her particular position, yet agency management wants to keep the individual within the agency. A way to make this happen and at the same time to assuage the individual's feelings is to give the person a new title. Yet, the new title can cause confusion since it may not reflect the person's true responsibilities. The final result is disruption and politics within the agency.

For example, a senior creative individual might reach a point where the day-to-day demands of his or her responsibilities are too much to handle. If the agency elects to place the individual in a new staff advisory role, the results could be negative. If the new role responsibilities are not clearly defined and if the new role's position within the agency structure is not known, a once valuable person can become a drain upon the agency. A better solution is to place the individual in another line position, most likely with less responsibility and less seniority than the former position. If this is not practical, working out a separation is better than allowing the individual to function within a role that has no real purpose in the agency. When creating a new position or title within the agency, need must override other considerations.

Another reason for false promotion is to keep an important individual from leaving the agency. Thus, in addition to the other means of keeping and rewarding an individual, a new, loftier sounding title is bestowed on the person. Unless this greater title is accompanied by greater responsibility, the agency is ill-served. The CEO, with the operations committee, should diligently police title changes. If not, over time the agency will suffer from title proliferation and puffery. This syndrome, which is readily observed in an agency, is a clear signal of deeper problems and an overall lack of strong management.

AGENCY MATRIX

The unique matrix organization of an advertising agency has been proven effective over time. The matrix consists of the basic product group system encompassing the line operatives from the various functions (account management, creative, media, and research) and the departmental system, which consists of the same functions noted before. The agency individual is both part of a department consisting of his or her specialty and of one or more product groups whose function is to perform for a given client. It is unlikely that this basic system can be improved. Normally, the individual is physically housed within his or her own department, which is where he or she also receives training, evaluation, and rewards. However, on a day-to-day basis the individual operates within the given product groups to which he or she is assigned.

Over the years, various experiments in housing people according to product group rather than by department have been tried. These arrangements seem only to work when the account is sizeable enough to justify 100 percent commitment of time of a large number of individuals. If a number of people are assigned to a given account, it does make sense to place them together physically. The truth of the matter is, the work in an agency gets done by product groups, not by departments. Yet, people are

housed within their departments and are loyal to the departments, where the recognitions and rewards tend to originate.

For this reason, it is important that cross-checks on individuals' performances are done. With such checks, the individuals'
true value as members of product groups is assessed, not just
their value as members of departments. Too often, departmen-
talism takes over and an individual is rewarded more on the
basis of his or her functional superiors' opinions than on what
the product group members think. The product group is closer to
the client since the group is responsible for the management of
the client's business.

THE EXECUTIVE FLOOR

Every agency has an executive floor housing the CEO and the key
people within the agency. The individuals making up the executive floor are a clear indication of the CEO's attitude and direction of the company. If the group is composed of staff people,
lawyers, and accountants, this says that the lawyers and accountants are playing a major role in running the agency. If, on the
other hand, it is composed of senior account, creative, and new
business operatives, clearly another message is being conveyed
about the agency, this one positive. This message says the agency
is being run by people involved in the creation and selling of
advertising, which is what the agency business is essentially
about. The management of the agency should never underesti-
mate the degree to which the entire agency is interpreting and
responding to the signals being given by the executive floor,
including factors such as the size, style, decor, and proximity of
the offices to the CEO's office. Executive floor watchers have been
known to literally measure office sizes to help determine who has
the most prestigious job. Of course, the closer the office to the
CEO's office, the more important the position.

LEVELS

When too many people are involved in the advertising approval
process, the advertising product is diminished. The more people

who have the opportunity to critique the work, whether members of the agency or of the client's operation, the more the central idea of the work will suffer. Operating levels add people to the approval process.

The number of levels that can become involved in the advertising review process are almost endless. At the agency, for example, there easily could be three review levels in the creative department (writer/art director, creative supervisor, associate creative director), three in account management (account executive, account supervisor, management supervisor), plus a whole host of management people (creative director, group director, office management, such as the director of client services), and even a creative review board for a total of 10 approval steps. All these precede the client's examination of the work, which could involve up to four or five approval levels. While the advertising business does not normally provide the time for all these levels to get involved in the process, many levels do, much to the detriment of the creative product.

The truth is, very few levels are actually needed to generate quality work, assuming the original idea has merit. Someone at the agency is needed to oversee the work to make sure it does have merit, that it is on strategy, and that it is of high quality from an executional standpoint. Account management should provide helpful input during the developmental process, not criticism at the end of the process. A good account management team is continually aware of the status of advertising under development. Finally, an agency overview at the highest level is necessary for quality control. This involves either the creative director and/or a creative review board.

Smart clients keep the advertising approval process down to two levels. This does not rule out attendance by other levels at approval meetings, but does limit their involvement in the process. The client organization should pass agency work through to the senior client levels as soon as possible to ensure that a good idea is accepted quickly and to prevent a bad idea from staying around for too long.

It is unfortunate that organizational levels, particularly in advertising agencies, ever came into existence. The agency business is simple. It requires some people to generate ideas and some to sell it to clients.

Why, then, are there all these levels? In account management, a major reason levels have been created is to duplicate client hierarchies in order to provide an agency counterpart for each client. The results have been a cumbersome system with much duplication and wasted effort and certainly a negative effect on the quality of advertising.

If the client's product management system contains the titles of product assistant, assistant product manager, associate product manager, product manager, and group product manager, with each responsible for managing a brand, it is conceivable (and actually has happened) that the agency has matched the five client levels with five account management operatives of its own. Any number of projects, assignments, and meetings can be created just to keep everyone busy. Busy people, however, are not necessarily productive. If an advertising idea gets caught in this maze, it most likely will not survive.

In the creative department, part of the reason levels have been generated is also client-driven: clients have demanded more and more that creative people be part of the selling process. As the work moved higher through the client organization, a more senior agency creative individual was demanded at each level. More of a factor in the generation of levels within creative departments is the proliferation of titles to keep people through "promotion" and to assuage egos. If a few agencies add a new title, oftentimes this title (i.e., new level) is adopted throughout the agency business. A more recent and confusing example is the use of the title "creative director" at a level removed from the top. Clients can now have this "creative director" in many more meetings since there may be half a dozen or more agency people with titles connoting creative director.

The only answer to these confusing and negative level escalations is for agency management to evolve to a simpler structure for the long term, while in the short term acting in the following two ways. First, simplify the agency approval process by permitting only one creative overview level within the operating levels of the agency and one final creative review level at the top of the agency. Hopefully, limiting review and approval to two levels will positively influence the advertising. Second, agency management must insist on a reduction in the client levels participating in the approval of agency creative work, and on a reduction in the time period before senior client levels see the work. Hastening the review process will improve the advertising. For example, the first client approval point might be at the group product manager level. All client levels prior to group product manager would attend one meeting to comment on the work. The group product manager, however, would make the decisions. The work then would proceed to the second and final approval level, say that of the marketing director.

WORLDWIDE COORDINATION

For multinational agencies, the need to effectively coordinate brand activities across national borders will increase over time because multinational companies are recognizing the need to disseminate knowledge and to coordinate international marketing activities. These companies will demand more from their agencies in these activities. At a minimum, they will want a senior agency executive to have worldwide responsibility for their worldwide brands.

An important adjunct of this issue is that the growth of agencies operating in one or just a few countries will be restricted by their inability to broadly coordinate activities. In the worst circumstances, these agencies will lose multinational brands and clients. As a result, these smaller agencies may need to merge with larger agency networks.

Some clients have recognized for many years the need to coordinate marketing on a multinational scale. This has been true whether or not many of these marketing efforts could indeed be duplicated in every country. What has been recognized by these pioneers is, that even if cultures vary considerably in response to a given brand's efforts and even to the brand itself, there still are lessons to be shared. These pioneers also realized that what is true in one country might later become true in another country. In either case, the communication of marketing experience throughout the company's system could lead to marketing successes and avoidance of failure duplication.

It is interesting to observe how parts of the world respond to different products over time. For example, in the case of decaffeinated coffee, one country, such as the United States, might reach the stage where 30 percent of the coffee consumed is decaffeinated, while in Sweden the amount might be 5 percent. Yet, the motivations for drinking decaffeinated coffee (essentially health related) are the same for the Swede as for the American. Swedish citizens, while coffee loving, are not yet as concerned about caffeine as are Americans. In marketing, lessons learned in the United States can be applied later in Sweden, as well as in all coffee-consuming countries.

Fast-food restaurants, such as McDonald's, have only lately been introduced to some parts of the world. Yet, the lessons learned in the more mature countries, such as the United States, can be applied to these later developing countries. Hence, the need exists for worldwide coordination by both the company and the advertising agency.

When consumers throughout the world approach the same goods and services similarly, as the media become more "worldly," as countries reduce restrictive laws and procedures (e.g., Europe, 1992), and as multinational companies grow and proliferate, so, too, must agencies become more international in their approach to brands. Compounding these changes is the recognition by companies that their brand names are precious equities to be managed as carefully as any other important asset. In addition to top management sensitivity toward these changes, agencies must structure themselves to meet the international needs of their clients. Several aspects of this process deserve attention.

First, individuals who are knowledgeable, experienced, and uniquely skilled in the demands of multinational brands must be members of the highest levels of the agency, some must hold rank at the executive vice-president level. These people should be recognized as being part of the senior level of agency management because they are, first of all, deserving of this rank, but also because they signal to the agency and clients alike that the agency takes multinational brand management seriously.

Second, agencies must create the clear impression that being part of multinational brand coordination and management is important to the agency, that there are clear career opportunities and paths available to those choosing these responsibilities, and that in no way are members of this part of the agency second-class citizens. This can only be done by rewarding multinational coordinators and managers with titles and monetary compensation equal to other senior executives within the agency.

Third, agencies must devote time and money to the training of individuals in the mechanics and subtleties of multinational brands. As part of this, agencies must assign people to overseas markets early in their careers so that they can learn firsthand about international brands from the perspectives of different countries. An individual who has worked on the same brand, say, in three countries, will bring the unique understanding required by this activity in the future.

Agencies that can effectively aid their clients in multinational brand management will be greatly rewarded. The stakes are large, but the rewards are commensurate.

In order to visualize agency organization, refer to the two prototypical organizational structures shown in Exhibits 3–1 and 3–2. Exhibit 3–1 outlines the structure of a single agency unit, say a $50 million agency with just one office. Exhibit 3–2 depicts the structure of a large, worldwide agency.

EXHIBIT 3–1
Diagram of an Agency Consisting of a Single Office

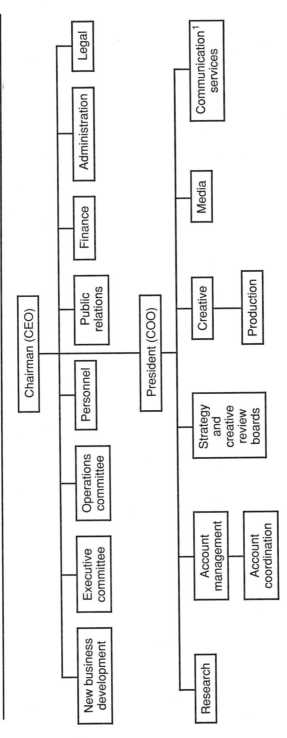

1. Includes such services as sales promotion, direct marketing, design, yellow pages, etc.

EXHIBIT 3–2
Diagram of a Worldwide Agency

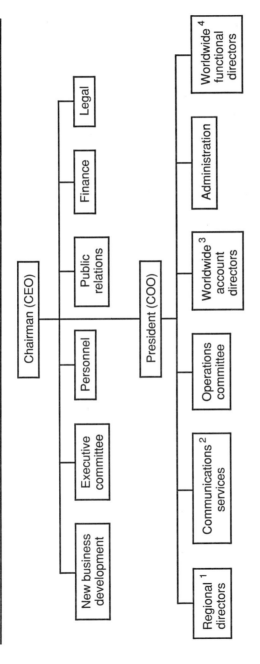

1. Individuals responsible for geographic parts of the world. All individual operating offices report here.
2. All allied services such as sales promotion, direct marketing, public relations, design, medical and/or yellow pages.
3. Senior executives in charge of worldwide accounts.
4. Senior worldwide creative, media and research individuals.

CHAPTER 4

PEOPLE

One way to examine an advertising agency is to look at the three Ps: people, product, and profits. People determine the quality of the product, and the product determines the quality of the profits. Not surprisingly, everything starts with the people. If management has not properly planned and organized the functions related to people management, the agency will not prosper. This chapter deals with the activities related to people management. They fall into five categories:

Hiring.
Training.
Evaluating.
Rewarding.
Retiring/Firing.

HIRING

Of the five people management activities, the hiring function is the most important. It is the biggest determinant of the quality of the agency's personnel. As will be shown, to derive the greatest benefit, there must be a clear delineation between the responsibilities of the centralized or corporate personnel function and those of the individual departmental personnel functions. Most importantly, the individual departments, not the centralized personnel function, must have final control of hiring individuals within the departments. For example, the account management department should hire the account managers.

The role of the corporate or centralized personnel function vis à vis the individual departments must be clear to everyone in order to avoid duplication and confusion. Basically, the corporate personnel group should be small and dedicated to those areas that by definition are universal to the personnel needs of the entire agency. These universal needs relate to benefits, vacations, holidays, hours, and sick days, as well as to issues involving compliance with government regulations. Any personnel issue affecting all the people within the agency should be part of the centralized personnel function. In the case of hiring, the role of the corporate function should be quite limited, perhaps just to the hiring of secretaries and receptionists.

Each department within the agency must be responsible for hiring its own people, and each department must have an individual whose primary if not total responsibility is hiring. That individual and all those in the department who become involved in the hiring process must be completely familiar with the jobs for which people will be hired. For example, in account management, those involved in hiring someone for an account executive position must have firsthand experience as an account executive if they are to be effective in this role. A prospective employee wants to meet and talk with individuals who are completely familiar with the job he or she is pursuing. An interview with a corporate personnel individual who has never been an account executive can make a negative impression on the prospective employee. Too often, agencies consider the interview to be a screening or approval process for the agency— a way for a privileged few to join the agency. They tend to forget the important fact that the interviewing process is also the way to attract and entice the best people to join the agency.

The same organization and process for hiring are used throughout the agency; for illustration, however, the example of the account executive is continued. There are a number of activities within the account management department that must be conducted as part of the hiring process. First, a designated individual must be the initial contact for all prospective employees, whether these initial contacts are by mail, referral, or agency recruitment efforts. As the initial contact, this individual should be responsible for communicating with prospective employees from the start through to the end of the process. All employment inquiries to the agency must receive a written response, whatever the possibilities might be for the individual's employment. The central hiring person in account management will develop a feel for the entire marketplace as the result of dealing with many prospects over a period of time.

Once an individual has qualified for an interview, at least four members of account management should meet one-on-one with him or her. Since interviewing of potential account executives is a year-round activity in most agencies, a large number of agency staff members must be skilled in the art of interviewing. These individuals, whatever their positions in account management, must be able to not only effectively interview and evaluate prospects, but they must also be outstanding at selling the agency to prospects. They must be agency ambassadors and cheerleaders if the agency hopes to attract the best account executives in the market. To assist the process and to ensure that all agency individuals are operating from a common perspective, an interview form must be prepared for all key functions. Exhibit 4–1 shows such a form, this for the account executive function.

EXHIBIT 4–1
Prospective Employee Evaluation Form (Account Executive)

1. Does the prospect have the necessary academic and intellectual qualifications to be an account executive?
2. Does the prospect have the related work experience necessary to the role of account executive?
3. Has the prospect held a leadership position or demonstrated leadership qualities in the past?
4. Does the prospect have the necessary communication skills (written or oral) to be an account executive?
5. Has the person demonstrated in the past an ability to work effectively with people?
6. Does the individual's personal appearance meet the requirements of the account executive role?
7. Assess the overall potential (outstanding, good, fair, poor) of the individual as an account executive.

The individual charged with the hiring function must coordinate the interviewing process and oversee the training of agency people in interviewing skills. This person must also analyze the results of all the interviews to arrive at a consensus regarding each candidate.

Once the hiring process is completed, the process of indoctrinating the new employee is initiated. Indoctrination can be divided into three parts. The first, which should be a role of the central personnel department, is to brief the new employee on all matters related to personnel policy. This includes basic information on such matters as benefits, vacations, holidays, and work hours.

The second aspect of indoctrination is a briefing of the agency in general. This briefing can include company brochures, slide presentations, examples of advertising and hopefully, a visit with a member of top management. The object of this phase is to give the new employee a perspective on the agency—its mission, clients, size, scope, and work.

The third part of indoctrination is conducted by the hiring department itself and relates to the department and the individual's role within it. Much of this part of indoctrination will have been accomplished as part of the interviewing process. The goal is to get the new employee off to an effective and quick start.

TRAINING

Indoctrination is really an early stage of agency training, a function that, if correctly organized, can positively impact the agency. The more effort an agency devotes to training, the stronger the agency will become. Employees not only perform better as a result of training, but they also feel better about themselves and about the company that provides the training. Therefore, it is advisable to insist that every employee, particularly those at the professional levels, participate in some form of training at least once a year.

Training must be organized so that the training activities that involve the entire agency staff are managed by a central training function. Individual departments should be responsible for those training activities related to their particular functions (as in the case of hiring).

At a minimum, a central function should exist for training in writing and verbal presentation skills. Training should also involve the agency's strategic development process. This training is essential for all new employees so that they can quickly speak the agency's strategic system language.

Managerial training in management skills, behavior, and attitudes, both internal and external, should be considered. There is an enormous variety of outside courses available both from the 4As (American Association of Advertising Agencies) and from the Association of National Advertisers, as well as from the business schools. This type of training is not only a means of professional advancement, it is also a way to signal to employees that they are recognized as being important to the future of the company. As such, this kind of training becomes a special reward to individuals.

Each department should assign the training function to one member. This training manager must create, manage, and monitor the training function within the department, while coordinating activities with the other departmental training managers and the central training function.

EVALUATING

All professional-level employees should be evaluated once a year. People need to know where they stand, and the company needs to periodically assess personnel quality.

Evaluation usually includes a job description form used in conjunction with a job evaluation form. The job description should be given to the new employee the first day on the job so the employee knows what is expected of him or her. Similarly, the job evaluation form should be made available to the employee early on so that he or she is aware of judging criteria. Prototypical job description and job evaluation forms for an account executive are shown in Exhibits 4–2 and 4–3. It is important that these forms are kept to a workable length and that they are updated periodically to reflect changes in the working environment.

EXHIBIT 4–2
Job Description (Account Executive)

The account executive, as a representative of the account management function within the agency, is a principal member of the product group having responsibility for developing and selling ideas to the client. Specific tasks include the following:

- Assist in the strategy development process.
- Oversee and coordinate all media, creative, and research activities.
- Manage day-to-day product group activities.
- Participate in the agency-client communication process on a day-to-day basis.
- Be responsible for reports and procedures related to budget control.
- Prepare conference and status reports.

To effectively accomplish these tasks, the account executive must acquire certain skills, as follows:

- Effective oral and written communication.
- Excellent organizational skills.
- Leadership strengths.
- Strong interpersonal skills.
- Analytical abilities.

The evaluation should be a two-way process, allowing the employee to react to the evaluation. The process must also include very specific follow-up steps, mutually agreed upon by the employee and the supervisor. Comments about the individual's career path and potential are important. The results of the evaluation should be circulated to at least two levels above the individual being evaluated and should also be reviewed by departmental top management.

All departmental evaluations should be reviewed, department by department, function by function, by top management once a year to gain a perspective on the overall level of quality within the agency. For example, all of the account executive evaluations should be examined to determine the percentage of account executives receiving high, average, or low evaluations; to determine if enough account executives are ready for promotion; and to determine if training is adequate. Analysis of other levels in account management will provide top management with an overview of the department and will help set a course of action for strengthening the department. The same process should be completed for the creative, media, and research functions. This

EXHIBIT 4–3
Job Evaluation (Account Executive)

Job Evaluation

Name: *Title:*   *Date:*

---

1. Describe individual's overall performance in current assignment.
2. Using a four-point scale (excellent, good, fair, and poor) assess the individual's abilities related to the following tasks and responsibilities:

   Strategy development   _____
   Agency output   _____

            Creative   _____
            Media   _____
            Research   _____
            Budgets   _____

   Agency internal communication and coordination   _____
   Client relationships   _____

3. Using the same four-point scale assess the individual's abilities related to the following skills:

   Communication

            Written   _____
            Oral   _____

   Organizational   _____
   Leadership   _____
   Analytical   _____
   Interpersonal   _____

4. In which training program has the individual participated in the last 12 months? What training is suggested in the future?
5. How long has the individual been in his or her current assignment? How long should the individual continue in this assignment?
6. What is recommended as a next assignment for this individual?
7. What are the prospects, including timing, for promotion? How far can the individual progress in the agency?
8. Other comments:
9. Interviewee's comments:

---

will result in an agency overview, which then becomes part of the business planning process described in Chapter 2.

An additional and excellent evaluation technique is to examine all individuals within a specific job function (e.g., account executives) by ranking them from the best to the worst. This technique will aid the promotion and reward process and will also be helpful in the event the agency must reduce staff.

REWARDING

There are a number of ways management can reward employees. In addition to basic salary and bonus awards, options include stock awards, promotions, transfers (including office to office), training, and task force participation. Rewards should be given in conjunction with the evaluation process as an impetus to do better and, in particular, to improve the skills identified in the evaluation process as needing improvement.

Rewards and awards should be spaced over time to give the employee the clear impression that he or she is continually being observed and recognized. For example, it is not necessary to give an employee a salary increase at the same time a promotion is given.

When it comes to compensation, employees tend to be more concerned with the short term than with the long term. Because of this shortsightedness, it is management's responsibility to not only develop long-term programs for agency employees, but also to communicate the value and wisdom of these programs to the employees.

Current compensation should have as a major component a bonus based on recent performance. If the salary component of current compensation is a significant percentage of total compensation, management runs the risk of employee complacency. For professional-level employees, at least 20 percent of total current compensation should be a bonus. The higher the level of the individual in the agency, the greater the percentage of compensation that should be derived from bonus. Very senior people might, in a good year, receive half salary–half bonus compensation. The increased weighting toward bonuses not only helps motivate employees, but also gives management the needed flexibility to reward according to agency profitability. If a given year is particularly profitable, bonuses can increase. In a bad year, management can lower or eliminate bonuses and still have a profitable year. The key here is to avoid large salary increases year to year since it is extremely difficult to reduce these, and in a bad economic year, they can result in an operating loss. Employees should be made aware that salaries, while important, are the base; extra performance can result in extra compensation, and extraordinary performance will be rewarded in kind.

Nonmonetary awards can be powerful motivators as well. An award given for performance that is publicized within the agency can have a beneficial and lasting effect. It is important that these awards are based on quality of product so that management gives off the proper signals of what is important to it. Some examples of nonmonetary awards are an advertisement-of-the-month award, and a best client-business-building-idea award.

FIRING

The way an agency handles employee departures says much about the company. Whether a person retires or is fired, his or her peers and friends will be watching the process carefully.

It is essential that an employee with a degree of status or longevity with a company who is either retiring or leaving voluntarily is given some kind of a farewell, either on or off the premises. This is an opportunity for friends to say good-bye, but it also dignifies the relationship between the employee and the agency. Obviously, these send-offs can vary in size, depending on the individual. For example, a departing creative director deserves a large send-off.

It is also critical that employees who are fired are treated with courtesy. Too often this does not happen, which signals not only to the departing employee, but to all of his or her peers, that the company does not care about people. For example, if an employee is fired and told to be gone by noon that day, fear and ill will are engendered among the remaining employees.

If the agency's evaluation system is working properly, an employee should be alert to the fact that he or she has performance problems. If the individual has been evaluated in writing and in person every six months by his or her supervisor and has been told there are problems that need to be corrected, if efforts to better train an individual have been made but to no avail, if the employee has subsequently been told that the possibility of being fired exists, and if the employee has not had a salary increase or promotion in two or three years, then the employee should have some indication of where he or she stands. Nonetheless, the actual firing will be traumatic.

Today, the federal government and the various states have laws regulating employment, particularly employment of minorities. Age and sex discrimination laws also exist. Accordingly, an agency needs expert legal counsel, either from within or outside the agency, to ensure that these laws are not violated. This is the responsibility of the corporate personnel department since all employees are affected.

While it is the direct supervisor's responsibility to evaluate individuals, the supervisor's superior must be aware of these reports and of any problems with employees since the decision to fire is made by management. In a smaller agency—one under $50 million in billings—the president of the agency should know of any firing, not just from a business standpoint, but also from a legal standpoint. The president must assess whether such action could result in a lawsuit. In a larger agency, the department head would have to agree to any terminations.

If any agency is truly professional and careful in hiring people and carries out good programs for training, evaluating, and rewarding its employees, then, hopefully, there will be little need to fire people.

QUALITIES OF THE ULTIMATE CREATIVE DIRECTOR

Other than the head of the agency, the most important person in an agency is the creative director since this individual has the greatest impact on the agency's basic product: its ideas. Because this position is so important, an agency should seek an individual who approaches the ideal. What qualities does the *ultimate* creative director possess?

First of all, the ultimate creative director believes in advertising strategy. He or she is convinced that strategic focus is essential to effective advertising. He or she believes that research and the time to absorb and analyze this research is fundamental to a successful advertising strategy. He or she does not look at, accept, or try to sell advertising that does not have a strategic framework.

The ultimate creative director is constantly seeking excellence in the agency output. He or she is relentless in communicating to employees that excellence is the ticket to success; that anything less is only grudgingly accepted; that the agency's obligation is to provide the very best creative product to its clients; that expediency is absolutely out of the question; and that the agency has a commitment to its creative product that cannot be compromised.

The ultimate creative director is selfless. He or she is willing to bestow credit where it belongs. He or she looks for employee collaboration and sponsors teamwork so that all can share in the success of the agency.

The ultimate creative director is an effective salesperson. He or she is able to sell management on the need for the right creative environment, on the need for fair employee compensation, and on the need for systems and procedures that enhance creativity. He or she can sell the clients on the advertising product and is constantly selling the agency as being a champion of creativity.

The ultimate creative director has managerial talent. He or she knows how to structure and organize the creative department to its best advantage. He or she understands the need for clear lines of responsibility, as well as the importance and effective use of rewards.

The ultimate creative director is creative in his or her own right. He or she has established a reputation for being creative. He or she is able to continue, if needed, to demonstrate this ability to create. The people respect this person, not only as a manager and a champion of creativity, but also as a creative individual.

The ultimate creative director provides direction. He or she is able to work with creative people to help them improve their product; he or she is not just someone who says yes or no to whatever is presented. At every creative meeting that this person attends, he or she provides input or direction that improves the creative product.

The ultimate creative director is a workaholic. He or she is obsessive in attention to the people and to the work they produce. He or she recognizes that each ad contributes to the total output of the agency and that his or her part in nurturing each ad is essential. He or she also recognizes that the creative director is the most important individual in the entire agency, and he or she acts as such.

The ultimate creative director is a trainer. He or she is able to teach people not just by example, but by instruction. The ultimate creative director considers two of his or her most important responsibilities to be the guidance and training of young people to not only make them better, but to enhance the reputation of the agency.

HOW TO SUCCEED IN A BIG AGENCY

What are the ways, in addition to hard work, to get ahead in an agency, particularly in a big agency? Variety is one of the advantages of being employed in the advertising business— variety of accounts, variety of people, variety of experiences. People on the rise in an agency should seek such variety. They should avoid being typecast as an individual suited to certain kinds of accounts, such as packaged goods, fast foods, auto, airline, or any of the many other client descriptions. Agency management will try to keep people in place as long as the client is happy. Therefore, individuals can find themselves fixed in place on an account long past the time when experience suggests a change. In other situations, individuals are moved from account A to account B, both accounts being essentially alike (for example, from an insurance agent to a financial service account). Client B is told someone with relevant experience is being assigned to the account, in this case, the person who handled client A's account. This behavior, if extended, can result in individuals being unnecessarily limited in experience, thereby retarding their growth. A third example is found in the travel sector, where a person becomes typecast as an airline, rental car, and/or tourism specialist. In the worst possible scenario, a person can be kept on a particular piece of business for an extended time. If the account is lost, the individual can be out of work.

Therefore, people on the way up should seek a variety of experiences, certainly including packaged goods, but also clients with other product lines, as well as clients from the service sector. Since this is the information age, experience with clients in the information field, such as a computer manufacturer, is also advised.

Employees of large agencies should carefully observe the career paths of the senior agency executives for ideas on how to plan their own career paths. The kinds of accounts the senior people were assigned, the jobs they held, and the offices in which they worked are all factors to be considered. If the agency's senior management has generally had overseas assignments, up-and-comers should seek similar jobs. If, for example, the London office has been a stepping stone for a number of people, an assignment in London might be a wise career move.

The majority of senior management in the big agencies started in the account management function. Usually, there is only one upper management member who has risen from the other functions (media, creative, research, finance). Therefore, the chances of reaching the senior management level are greatly enhanced by pursuing a career in account management.

A rising executive can further his or her career by working on the agency's major account. Not only will the experience be valuable, but the visibility will help. Top management necessarily will watch the biggest account more closely.

A good way to get additional experience and exposure is to participate in agency task forces. All agencies rely on task forces to periodically analyze agency problems. Often these groups prepare and present recommendations to management. Involvement with a task force provides a unique opportunity to work with a different group of people within the agency. It can also be a valuable learning experience, as when management assigns a task force to recommend ways to make the agency more streamlined organizationally. By participating, each member meets other agency employees, learns about organization, and becomes better acquainted with management. The fact that task force endeavors are conducted over and above the basic job is another bonus. Management will appreciate the extra effort.

The sooner an individual achieves profit-and-loss responsibility, the sooner he or she will rise in the agency, assuming, of course, endeavors meet with success. In an agency, there are a large number of people who have proven themselves effective at managing accounts, but in all the big agencies, few individuals have proven they can successfully manage a profit center. Therefore, ambitious young people should seek profit center opportunities early—no matter how small. Running a small branch office is one such opportunity. It is important that these newcomers prove to senior management early in their careers that they are capable of running an autonomous profit center.

Many of these suggestions apply to careers in medium-sized agencies. However, early experience with a big agency is recommended. It is easier to trade big agency experience for a job in a smaller agency that it is to move from a small agency to a big one.

CHAPTER 5

AGENCY PRODUCT

An advertising agency exists to produce ideas; these are the main products of the agency. A client hires an agency to get ideas. Agencies that create ideas that work will grow and profit because clients tend to increase budgets for such ideas.

Despite the importance of idea generation to agencies, most clients believe they are not getting the quality or the quantity of ideas they need from their agencies. They believe this because there is little evidence that their advertising is working for them in the marketplace. Sometimes there is no evidence that the advertising is clearly communicating something meaningful to the consumer; or sometimes there is no evidence that the consumer is thinking and behaving differently as a result of the advertising; or sometimes there is no evidence that a positive correlation exists between advertising and sales. In many cases, there is no evidence of any of these three advertising goals. Rarely is there evidence of all three.

Moreover, most clients are convinced that their agencies do not adequately understand their businesses in general and their marketing situations in particular and therefore cannot develop ideas that will truly build the business. Clients believe that too often agencies provide ideas that are not within the context of the client's marketing needs.

Agency management can do a number of things to improve the agency's creative product. This chapter covers those aspects of agency product that can be influenced and improved upon by agency management, thereby resulting in an overall improvement in creativity.

SYSTEMS WITHIN THE AGENCY

Many people argue against agency systems when it comes to the creative product. They believe that systems are the enemy of idea generation; they slow down the process and inhibit creative people. Some people are opposed to any systematic approach to creativity. Certainly, if an agency permitted its creative process to become overly systematic and bureaucratic, the result would be a reduction in the quantity and quality of its creative output. For example, if an agency became overly reliant on boards of review for either strategy or creative execution and/or the agency had an overly elaborate series of systems and procedures related to the creative development process, that agency could become so stultified that no good ideas would ever survive.

Nevertheless, a certain amount of process is essential to the creation of business-building ideas. Three elements are mandatory.

First, one mandatory element is a strategy document that contains the relevant information and focus necessary for creative people to develop advertising. The strategy document is one with which all agency personnel should not only be familiar, but also be trained in its use. The document should also be known to the agency's clients since the best advertising only results from the client's participation in the strategic part of the advertising development process. The next section of this chapter deals more fully with the subject of creative strategy.

A second mandatory element is an agency strategy review board. Many agencies have abandoned this element of the creative process in recent years, much to the detriment of their advertising product.

The purpose of the strategy review board is, first, to signal to agency personnel that the agency takes advertising strategy very seriously. Second, the strategy review board offers advice during strategy creation. The strategy review board does not merely approve or disprove strategies, rather, the board provides to the product group criticism and suggestions to improve the strategy. Accordingly, the board should consist of agency individuals most skilled in the development and evaluation of creative strategy.

To be most effective, the strategy review board should consist of a rotating group of the most senior and experienced individuals in the agency. This setup avoids the negative impressions associated with a permanent group. A permanent group can become too much of an institution, even political in nature.

A strategy review board should review the creative strategy on every agency brand at least once a year. If, at any time, a brand changes strategy, the new strategy should be presented to the strategy review board at that time.

The strategy review board also should be available on short notice so as not to impede the total creative development process.

The head of the strategy review board should be a senior member of agency management, someone who is also respected for his or her abilities in strategy development. Another senior manager should be responsible for monitoring the strategy review process to ensure compliance with agency objectives and procedures.

The third mandatory component of the creative development process, in addition to an effective creative strategy document and strategy review board, is a mechanism or procedure for reviewing the creative work itself. In many agencies, this probably is the responsibility of the creative director. Certainly, whatever the creative review process, the creative director must play a major role. An agency must have a strong quality control process if it expects its work to be of a high caliber. Allowing individual product groups to decide in their own right what ideas should be recommended to clients is a sure way to reduce quality for the sake of expediency. It must be remembered that account management, with whom clients have primary contact, is extremely interested in client approval of creative work. Faced with the inevitable time deadlines, account management may be willing to sell a lesser idea to the client just to get on with business, to make air dates, and to keep relationships friendly. Therefore, it behooves management to develop and enforce a creative review process that is consistent with top management's goals for the agency's creative output.

Effectively developed and working in tandem, a creative strategy document, a strategy review board, and a creative review process contribute to business-building advertising ideas.

CREATIVE STRATEGY

Fully half the problems that develop between an advertiser and the ad agency over creative effort can be traced back to an issue involving creative strategy. Put another way, there is a lack of understanding by one of the parties about just what the advertising in intended to accomplish. If everyone does not have a clear picture of the purpose of the advertising, it is no wonder that problems develop in evaluating the agency's efforts to implement the strategy. There are several causes for this strategic dilemma.

First, a statement of the advertising's purpose may not exist, whether this statement is termed "strategy," "objective," "goal" or another word that gets to the heart of the matter. However, situations where a statement does not exist are rare. More common is a statement of purpose or advertising strategy that is so poorly prepared, so lacking in insight, and so far removed from sound analysis of substantive consumer research and knowledge that it is worse than no statement at all. For if creative strategy is not founded on consumer understanding, formulated by experienced advertising professionals, and, finally, written clearly and incisively by the agency and client working as a team, then that strategy is not going to be the needed blueprint for effective advertising.

Another breakdown at the strategic level can occur even when a good strategic statement exists. This occurs when the working parties interpret the creative strategy differently. Particularly when dealing in words and phrases related to product imagery or personality, as opposed to product performance, there is a good chance of misinterpretation. If, for example, the strategy calls for the product to be shown in "youthful, modern, and feminine" environments, everyone had better understand just what these words mean and to what degree the brand will be shown to be young, up-to-date, and ladylike. This is why it behooves client and agency to spend a great amount of time discussing the strategic purpose of the advertising before anyone puts pencil to paper to create advertising for that strategy.

Therefore, clients and agencies must work within a strategy development process or system, such as that shown in Exhibit 5–1, that will lead to strong strategy statements. The strategy statement includes the pertinent information needed by creative people to create advertising. Since a good strategy statement is so essential to the creation of effective advertising, the statement should be as comprehensive as possible. Many agencies and a number of clients have their own proprietary strategy documents, many of which are quite good. The prototype shown in Exhibit 5–1 is a distillation of many, intended to show the necessary elements and to drop other less useful ones. Exhibit 5–1 includes 11 areas of information or direction, each of which is discussed in detail.

In order to better understand the prototypical creative strategy document shown in Exhibit 5–1, Exhibit 5–2 shows a blank document. Three imaginary examples of how the statement might look for three imaginary brands—a new wash-day product called Electro-Wash (see Exhibit 5–3), an existing children's colored pencil brand named Scribbles (see Exhibit 5–4), and an imported beer named Los Caballeros (Exhibit 5–5), which has been on the market for three years—are also provided.

EXHIBIT 5–1
Creative Strategy Document

Section 1: Historical Perspective

This section is a brief, historical perspective helpful to the creative individuals who will write advertising for the brand. Key facts about the brand—how it functions and how it is perceived by consumers—should be included. Recent marketing events relevant to the current advertising situation should also be included. A brief summary of the brand's current sales situation should be outlined.

Section 2: Brand Personality Definition

All brands have a brand personality. This is a description of a brand in human terms. The more successful the brand, the more defined its personality becomes. This section should take into account the existing brand personality and an idealized future personality.

Section 3: Executional Equity

Any equity in terms of executional elements the brand has from previous advertising campaigns should be included here. This could be a logo, a theme line, a musical heritage, a graphic look, and/or any other element that represents meaningful continuity of message to the consumer.

Section 4: Competitive Framework

What are the brands with which the brand will compete for consumer patronage? These should be listed in this section so the creative team has a clear perspective of the competition for consumer attention.

Section 5: Target Audience

A description in quantitative and qualitative terms of the target audience includes all demographic data, as well as any other relevant information on those likely to buy the product. Psychographic information is included here.

Section 6: Advertising Objective

A clearly stated, succinct objective statement of what the advertising is to accomplish should be included here.

Section 7: Advertising Promise

A brief set of words representing the essence of the promise the agency wants to make to consumers is included in this section.

Section 8: Support for Claims

All facts and related information supportive of the advertising strategy and promise should be included in this section.

EXHIBIT 5–1
(concluded)

Section 9: Mandatories

In this section, any legal or other requirements of which creative people should be aware in developing advertising for the brand are listed.

Section 10: Research Needs

Section 10 presents a short statement listing missing pieces of information that would help in developing advertising strategy. Since the strategic process is an evolving one, it is important to keep in mind the consumer information that would be helpful in improving strategy in the future.

Section 11: Intended Effects of the Advertising

Three subsections are included here: knowledge, perceptions, and behavior. In this section, a statement is made of the knowledge the consumer should gain as a result of the advertising, the changes in perceptions toward the brand that will result from the advertising, and the consumer behavioral changes that will result because of the advertising.

EXHIBIT 5–2
Creative Strategy Document

Full Brand Name:

1. Historical perspective:
2. Brand personality definition:
3. Executional equity
4. Competitive framework:
5. Target audience:
6. Advertising objective:
7. Advertising promise:
8. Support for claims:
9. Mandatories:
10. Research needs:
11. Intended effects of the advertising
    Knowledge:
    Perceptions:
    Behavior:

EXHIBIT 5–3
Creative Strategy Document

Brand Name: Electro-Wash

Section 1: Historical Perspective

Electro-Wash is the first wash-day product to clean electronically in water. The product cleans without the chemicals normally found in detergents (e.g., builders and surfactants). Electro-Wash has no chemicals and does not create suds or potentially harmful wastes; the product is considered ecologically pure. Because of its revolutionary nature and superior cleaning performance, the brand will be introduced nationally with the biggest advertising and promotional budget ever spent in the soap and detergent category.

Section 2: Brand Personality Definition

Since Electro-Wash is new, marketing efforts will be aimed at creating a strong personality for the brand. The basic elements of that personality are as follows: Electro-Wash is a male. Moreover, he is an extremely virile male, soldierly in appearance, heroic, fit, and independent. Electro-Wash is youthful and modern, completely with the times and, to a marked degree, futuristic in attitude. Electro-Wash makes women feel that he is in control of the situation, that only good things can happen when he is around and, therefore, women can have complete confidence in him.

Section 3: Executional Equity

As a new brand, Electro-Wash has no brand equity. A strong introductory logo does, however, exist. Research has shown this logo to be consistent with the product's known efficacy and desired brand personality. The logo should be prominent in all communication, particularly advertising.

Section 4: Competitive Framework

Electro-Wash is intended to compete with mainstream heavy-duty household detergents, both liquid and powder.

Section 5: Target Audience

The primary target for Electro-Wash is women, 30 to 45 years old, married, with children. Geographically, those women are spread proportionately to the usage of household detergents in the country. While both working and nonworking women are targets for the brand, working women in particular are believed to be more responsive to Electo-Wash's modern, scientific image. Also, people with septic tanks will be more receptive to Electro-Wash's claim of being ecologically pure. And while primarily women select and use detergents, men are more and more being recognized as a factor in this market, and the scientific nature of the brand could be of interest to a number of them.

EXHIBIT 5–3
(*concluded*)

Section 6: Advertising Objective

Advertising will convince women and some men that Electro-Wash is a new scientific breakthrough that provides superior cleaning without chemicals, suds, or ecological waste.

Section 7: Advertising Promise

Electro-Wash gets clothes cleaner than ever before and does so without chemicals, suds, or ecological waste.

Section 8: Support for Claim

Electro-Wash is the first wash-day product formulated to work electronically in water. Because it works electronically, Electro-Wash is the cleanest product ever developed.

Section 9: Mandatories

All advertising must include a visual demo illustrating how the product works. Strong logo identification also is required in all advertising messages.

Section 10: Research Needs

Periodic consumer usage and attitude data will be required, beginning with the introduction of Electro-Wash and every six months thereafter.

Section 11: Intended Effects of the Advertising

Knowledge

At the end of six months, it is expected that the target audience will be aware of the following to the degree shown:

• Brand name awareness.	95%
• Awareness that brand is a wash-day product.	90%
• Understanding of the unique way that Electro-Wash works.	75%

Perceptions

After six months, it is intended that the target audience will have the following perceptions to the degree shown:

• Believe that Electro-Wash is superior.	50%
• Believe that Electro-Wash is a breakthrough because of the way it works.	40%

Behavior

At the end of the first year, Electro-Wash will have achieved a 15 percent share of market as the result of a trial purchase rate of 30 percent and a repeat purchase rate of 50 percent.

EXHIBIT 5-4
Creative Strategy Document

Brand Name: Scribbles

Section 1: Historical Perspective

Scribbles are colored pencils for children. They have been on the market for five years, but have not achieved satisfactory sales. Recently the product has begun to lose distribution in key children's retail outlets. The product is unique. Scribbles are colored pencils that come in the form of wide ballpoint pens. They last longer than crayons (are more economical) and do not break like crayons. Yet, children either do not know or do not care about the advantages of Scribbles. As a result, crayons remain the dominant product in the market.

Section 2: Brand Personality Definition

Research indicates that children, while being aware of Scribbles, have a negative image of the brand. The brand's personality can be described as a person (neither male nor female), with a rather boring personality—older, practical, economical (perhaps cheap). In fact, Scribbles has the personality of a person most children do not identify as a friend. Advertising should alter the existing personality to make it younger, more fun, and friendlier.

Section 3: Executional Equity

Over the years advertising strategy and, thus, campaigns for Scribbles have changed almost annually. There has been no campaign continuity. Each campaign has had new music, new demonstrations, and new themes. As a result, there is no brand equity on which to draw.

Section 4: Competitive Framework

The primary competition for Scribbles is crayons. Another less formidable competitor is colored ballpoint pens.

Section 5: Target Audience

The main target for Scribbles is children aged 5 to 12. Scribbles's current business, as well as that of crayons, skews toward urban and country areas. Research shows that the more creative the child, the more frequently he or she uses Scribbles. This research also applies to crayons.

Section 6: Advertising Objective

Convince children that Scribbles is the fun product designed especially for creative children.

Section 7: Advertising Promise

Kids who use Scribbles have the most fun and are the most creative.

EXHIBIT 5–4
(*concluded*)

Section 8: Support for Claims

Scribbles last and last.

Section 9: Mandatories

None.

Section 10: Research Needs

A monthly tracking study among children is needed to measure awareness, usage, and perceptions of Scribbles.

Section 11: Intended Effects of the Advertising

Knowledge

Advertising should maintain the present high awareness level (85 percent) of Scribbles.

Perceptions

Advertising should increase positive perception levels of Scribbles on the following characteristics:

	Today	One Year From Today
Fun	5%	25%
For creative kids	8%	25%
The best	6%	15%

Behavior

Increase share of market from 10 to 15 percent. Increase unit sales by one third.

EXHIBIT 5–5
Creative Strategy Document

Brand Name: Los Caballeros

Section 1: Historical Perspective

Los Caballeros is the oldest and biggest imported Spanish beer, it is, in fact, the only significant brand from Spain. In the past year Los Caballeros increased sales by 12 percent and achieved a 5 percent share of the U.S. beer market.

Section 2: Brand Personality Definition

Los Caballeros has a very definite brand personality. This personality was established in its introductory advertising campaign and has remained consistent to date. The brand personality is essentially male. Moreover, this male works hard and plays hard; he is a tough individual, yet part of a team. This man is very attractive to women.

Section 3: Executional Equity

Los Caballeros is rich in executional equity. In addition to the Los Caballeros logo depicting a team of galloping horses, there is the well-known Los Caballeros music, and the brand's familiar theme line: Los Caballeros—For men who know and enjoy life. Virtually all Los Caballeros advertising has shown men in both work and romantic situations.

Section 4: Competitive Framework

Los Caballeros competes primarily with the premium-priced imported beer.

Section 5: Target Audience

The primary target for Los Caballeros is men aged 25 to 35, who are in the upper income levels, live in urban centers, and have a college degree. These men see themselves as rugged individualists and great lovers even though they tend to live rather sedentary and unromantic lives.

Section 6: Advertising Objective

Maintain and increase the Los Caballeros image as the premium beer for men who are both economically and romantically successful. Also maintain that Los Caballeros is a great-tasting beer.

Section 7: Advertising Promise

Los Caballeros: The beer for men who know.

EXHIBIT 5–5
(continued)

Section 8: Support for Claims

Los Caballeros is the beer made from the finest waters of Seville, Spain.

Section 9: Mandatories

All advertising must show the brand logo and the theme line. All broadcast advertising must include the brand's musical theme.

Section 10: Research Needs

An up-to-date usage and attitude study will be needed next year.

Section 11: Intended Effects of the Advertising

Knowledge

Maintain the brand's high awareness level (90 percent) among the target audience.
Raise the brand's theme line awareness from 65 percent to 80 percent.

Perceptions

Maintain the brand's perception as the leading beer for men who work hard and play hard.

Behavior

Increase share of market from 5 percent to 5.5 percent.
Increase unit sales by 10 percent.

ADVERTISING MEASUREMENTS

The mechanisms to evaluate advertising developed by American industry over the last 20 years did much to damage the quality of the creative product. The most widely used TV research method, day-after recall, had and still has several limitations. First, it does not measure the emotional effects of the advertising; it tends to focus on the rational side of the advertising. All brands have emotional elements, and many brands are almost totally emotional in their appeal, soft drinks being a good example. By concentrating its measurement on the rational, what-does-the-brand-functionally-do-for-me side of consumer satisfaction, day-after recall was handicapped from the start as a useful research vehicle.

A second liability of day-after recall research it its tendency to drive creative people to formula advertising. Clients and agencies alike have learned how to achieve high recall—experience showed that certain techniques and devices hyped recall. Creative people constructed commercials out of the individual building blocks known to work—product demonstrations, repeated arguments delivered in an overbearing fashion, and characters set in minidramas with the product as "hero." A whole school of look-alike advertising resulted. As the industry matured, consumers rejected these formalized commercials and with modern technology, even zapped them.

Another inherent problem with day-after recall, or any after-the-fact measuring tool, is that it comes toward the end of the advertising development process. Therefore, it tends to be punitive, not generative. It gives a pass-fail grade after most of the work has been done. Smart advertisers and their agencies are beginning to focus more research dollars on the generative front end of the process, deciding whether a core advertising idea fits the strategy and is understandable to the consumer before investing time and money in the production process.

From the start, advertisers recognized that recall testing mainly measured the early stages of the communication process. They knew, however, that persuasion and behavioral change were the desired end results of advertising. Unfortunately, the technologies developed and made available for the purpose of measuring behavioral change and persuasion were not predictive. Whether statistically sound or not, the question was, how do you relate a one-time exposure measurement to the long-term effectiveness of an advertising idea? You do not.

As a result, 20 years of great expense and effort have not provided the industry with research tools that are very helpful in predicting the effectiveness of advertising. Advertisers remain frustrated, not knowing whether their advertising investments will pay off. Agencies and clients alike have reduced research staffs and are less hopeful of ever achieving useful advertising research.

Agency managers can, however, take steps to reassure clients that there is value in their advertising. First and foremost, the client and the agency must work together to develop a meaningful advertising strategy. This means having sufficient and timely consumer research information from which intelligent strategic hypotheses can be drawn. It means having a creative strategy process and document that can serve as the blueprint for the creative product. It means having effective agency control systems, both at the strategic and at the executional stages of advertising development.

If these elements of the process are in order, agency and client alike will be more confident that the advertising is communicating within a meaningful consumer strategy, which is at least half the battle of business-building advertising. If the strategy is right, even an average advertising idea will have a positive effect in the marketplace, but even the most clever ideas will not move the business if the strategy is incorrect.

While there is hope for the development of better advertising strategy, there is less hope for developing the means for measuring the effectiveness of advertising. Because of the complexity of the human mind and the unpredictability of human behavior, it is unlikely that advertisers will ever be able to say with any certainty just how effective their advertising is.

CRITERIA OF GOOD ADVERTISING

In recent years, in addition to a trend away from the principles of effective advertising strategy, there have been two other trends that have worked against the creation of strong advertising ideas. One has been the reduction of time and effort for training, and the second has been the tendency to promote people more quickly.

As a result of these two trends, junior- and middle-level professionals in creative and account management oftentimes know very little about the basics of good advertising. With little or no knowledge of the basics, they have no way of evaluating work in process. If the client is equally unschooled, shoddy work gets through.

This book is concerned with agency management issues, not the building blocks of advertising per se. Moreover, there are many excellent books on the elements of advertising, the dos and don'ts of making advertisements. Nevertheless, there are some timeless advertising rules that bear repeating, even in this book's context, if only for the purpose of reminding agency managers that they can never assume that the professional staff is truly professional when it comes to making and evaluating advertising. Perhaps even the managers have forgotten the rudiments.

Following are some of these basic rules. These are questions to ask when examining an advertising idea.

- Is the advertising on strategy? Does it meet the criteria set down in the strategy document?
- Is the main idea of the advertising simple, believable, clear, memorable, and relevant?
- Is the advertising tailored to the brand? Could another brand or brands be substituted for the brand?
- Is the advertising consistent with the brand's personality?
- Does the advertising have the potential for longevity? Can it be pooled out? Can it be extended over time with a variety of creative executions?
- Does the advertising lend itself to other communication disciplines—sales promotion, direct marketing, public relations?
- Does the advertising include human benefits beyond the functional benefits of the brand? Does it clearly and positively portray the characteristics of the brand's user? Does it reach the consumer on an emotional level, as well as on an intellectual level?
- Does the advertising contain a demonstration of the brand's benefit?
- Are the visual and verbal elements of the advertising consistent with and supportive of each other? Can the visual and verbal elements stand alone?
- Are the arguments and benefits depicted supported by believable, meaningful information?
- Is the context of the advertising—its situation, its characters—meaningful, relevant, and believable?
- Are any of the elements of the advertising extraneous, irrelevant, confusing, or in opposition to the main selling idea?

Most advertisements cannot live up to these standards; few receive "yes" answers to all these questions. Therefore, it behooves advertising managers to acknowledge to themselves and to stress to their staff the need for adherence to some basic advertising guidelines that have been proven over time, such as these. No set of rules can substitute for quality strategy development and review, an experienced and trained professional staff, and the raw generation of innovative ideas, but they can improve the quality of an agency's output. If nothing else, rules can eliminate some bad advertising before it sees the light of day.

ASPECTS OF THE CREATIVE PROCESS

The most important determinant of an agency's creative quality is its creative talent. Accordingly, one of the highest management priorities is to improve the talent in this area. Whether or not this priority is met, management and staff can still produce quality advertising if other dimensions of the creative process are improved. These dimensions are *strategic focus, immersion, collaboration, agency environment, responsibility,* and *rewards*.

The lack of *strategic focus* is the primary cause of ineffective advertising. As stated earlier, in recent years agencies have strayed from using strategy as the foundation for good advertising for several reasons. Clients have reduced their emphasis on the fundamental research necessary to formulate intelligent strategy. They have also become less reliant on agencies for marketing and advertising strategy advice. There are fewer true client-agency marketing partnerships than in the past. Whereas at one time agencies were totally involved in marketing planning—even writing the plan in many instances—today agencies have little involvement in marketing planning.

It is also worth restating that as clients have reduced agency compensation in one way or another, agencies, in order to maintain profit margins, have reduced labor costs in the functions where marketing and strategic insights are most likely to originate—research and account management. Ten years ago agencies hired starting account managers at levels equal to those paid by clients to entry-level product managers. Today this is no longer true. Therefore, the quality of account management, particularly its ability to provide clients with quality marketing and advertising advice, has declined.

In research, the about-face from substantive quantitative investigation to more qualitative, seat-of-the-pants research has reduced the level of strategic insight. The raw data are not available for analysis.

The acceleration of the whole process has resulted in a more expedient attitude on the part of the agency: get the advertising approved, produced, and on the air so as to move on to the next project. All of this has been compounded by unusually high employee turnover within the agency and within the client's organization. This reduces the continuity necessary for solid strategic development. As recently as a decade ago people would be assigned to brands for years. Now, months are more typical assignment lengths.

Because so much instability has developed in recent years, an agency absolutely must have an effective strategic process. This will serve as the foundation for advertising that works.

A second aspect of the creative process that can be improved is *immersion*. Creative people must have the data, the means, and, importantly, the time to totally immerse themselves in the advertising problem. Solid strategy development can greatly short-circuit this process, but creative people need to be extremely knowledgeable of the product or service, the competition, and the relevant retail situation. They also must have access to all the consumer information available. This immersion in data will enable these people to produce ads that work. Continuity in assignments will provide the time for immersion. It is not surprising that in times of crisis the best advertising solutions are suggested by the creative people closest to the situation, not by those called in on short notice to solve the problem.

Contrary to popular opinion, most agency ideas are a *collaborative* effort. It has been found that the longer people work together, the more likely they are to create ideas. As people get to know each other better, they communicate more openly and are less fearful that their ideas will be rejected.

Agency management must recognize that collaboration is an important aspect of the creative process and provide for the continuity that leads to better collaboration. Keeping overall turnover of creative personnel in the area of 15 percent or less per year, maintaining consistent management, and keeping people on assignments for a prolonged period of time are three ways to enhance collaboration.

Another aspect of the creative process that has a powerful effect on creative quality is the agency's *environment*. Agency environment includes the cultural, physical, and managerial factors affecting the creative process. If the history of the agency is rich in creativity, this will assist the creative process. If the physical layout and the ambience of the agency are conducive to good communication, creativity will be enhanced. If the management behaves as though creativity is of great importance, creative people will react positively to these signals. Improvement of the environment should be a never-ending management task.

One way to improve the creative environment is to display advertising in the reception areas, hallways, and conference rooms. If the agency has won creative awards, prominently display these, too. Since advertising is an artist's endeavor, show a variety of art forms. Make the environment physically warm, bright, lively, and fun. Make it easy for people to interact by providing facilities for such activities as eating, exercising, watching movies, and training. Bring in interesting guest speakers, and throw parties, particularly to celebrate creative endeavors.

The more clearly management can define *responsibility* within the creative process, the better the results will be. People respond to clear responsibility and are confused by fuzziness. The further down in the organization that management can define responsibility, the better the system will respond. Make writers, art directors, and account executives believe that they are responsible for specific advertisements. Where responsibility is unclear, lapses will occur. Every brand, every campaign, and every advertisement should be clearly assigned to individuals so that at every level in the creative department it is known where the responsibility lies. If specific individuals are not assigned responsibilities, then no one will be and, as expected, results will be poor.

The final aspect of the creative process that management can positively affect is *rewards*. Rewards come from many sources and in a variety of forms. It is management's responsibility to see that credit is given where (and when) credit is due.

Economic rewards should be linked to creative successes so that it is clear that creativity is the agency's purpose. Noneconomic rewards, which can come from within the agency, from clients (if they are smart), or from the industry, should be celebrated, publicized, and acknowledged by management as important events. Management's recognition can create a bandwagon effect, leading to even greater levels of creativity. For example, management can establish a small cash fund for instant rewards. Monthly or annual awards for the best ideas can be instituted. The press can be invited to celebrations of creative breakthroughs.

In summary, there are a number of manageable aspects of the creative process that can be improved, resulting in a better creative product. Again, these aspects are solid strategic focus, immersion, collaboration, the creative environment, assignment of clear responsibilities, and creative awards.

WHAT'S THE BIG IDEA?

No one can be in the agency business for very long, certainly not in a position involving client contact, without having the client ask for a "big idea." The higher the client level, the more insistent the cry for big ideas, and the greater the incidence of a client's prior association or experience with a successful advertising campaign, the greater that client's desire for another success.

A big idea is to a client just that—advertising that will have a positive impact on the client's business. This is the reason the agency was hired in the first place. While many factors other than advertising exist within marketing (product, price, distribution, package, promotion, trade factors, and competition, to name the most important) intelligent, experienced clients know that a successful "big idea" advertising campaign can catapult their businesses ahead. Since business-building advertising does not cost a client any more than ineffective advertising, the leverage on the upside of a successful advertising campaign is enormous. Viewed in this way, advertising is for the client a potential source of increased productivity.

This chapter, in an effort to provide insights into ways of improving an agency's creative product, has described the processes necessary to the creation of effective advertising, has explored the role of advertising research measurements, has described the criteria of good advertising, and has outlined the various aspects of the creative process conducive to idea generation. This last section deals with the *knowledge* and *mentality* individuals and agencies in total need to create big ideas which are what clients seek.

Knowledge is one of the keys to the creation of big ideas. First, an individual must have knowledge of advertising skills. This knowledge should be gained early in an individual's career. Second, the individual must have knowledge of the consumer and human beings in general. Advertising is very much intertwined with human psychology. The more that is known about the human mind and about human behavior, the more successful the advertising.

Next, knowledge of the specific consumer, the target audience for the brand to be advertised, should be gained. For most brands, there is an existing body of information about the consumer; often there is industrywide data. This can be supplemented by individual interviews with consumers. Hearing consumers speak in their own words about the brands they use can be most helpful to advertising people.

Knowledge of the product or service to be advertised is critical to the big idea. Going to the factory or the service center, understanding the competition, and personally using the product or service are all necessary to truly understanding the advertising assignment.

Knowledge of the client—history, people, organization, systems, and attitudes—is also a necessary ingredient to the creation of a successful campaign.

Finally, knowledge in general is needed for effective advertising. The more an individual knows about different subjects, the more information he or she has to solve an advertising problem.

It is obvious that an astute advertising professional is constantly adding to his or her knowledge. Acquiring this knowledge, however, requires hard work. The more time spent learning about a consumer, a product, or a client, the more knowledgeable an individual becomes. Therefore, those who do their homework will benefit directly from their efforts.

Less measurable and less attainable are those attributes or mentalities that can be acquired by people—mentalities that can make a person a better communicator and, therefore, someone more capable of developing big ideas. For example, the ability to think like the consumer helps in the creation of a big idea. This goes beyond knowing what a consumer is seeking in a product category. It involves understanding the complete mind-set of the consumer so that the words and pictures in the advertising are just right. To a degree, this is a function of having "street smarts" as opposed to "book smarts." It is a mentality obtained from having lived with the people who represent the particular target audience. The more varied the experiences with people an individual has had, the more varied the brands for which he or she is likely to develop successful advertising.

Another mentality that is important to developing ideas is being able to put on a business hat—to truly go inside the clients' minds. What do the clients really think about their businesses, and what do they hope for in this context from the advertising? Short of having been in a business situation themselves, advertising professionals can only obtain this mentality through prolonged interaction with clients. Clients are particularly astute in detecting advertising people who have this business sense or mentality.

An ability to persevere with an idea is also essential to the creation of big ideas. As has been noted, there are a number of systems, research mechanisms, and levels of people within both the agency and the client's organization that are capable of destroying an idea. Unless someone believes in the idea and has the conviction to stand by the idea so that it survives more or less intact, no big ideas will emerge. People who come by this trait naturally or who have developed it over time will have a much better chance of producing big ideas.

Few people have been successful at idea generation without a sense of humor. It is, unfortunately, a trait people either have or do not have. A sense of humor is necessary to relieve the day-to-day tensions of the advertising business. Humor can also enhance the actual advertisement. Consumers respond to humor in advertising as long as it is relevant to the selling idea. Humor that is irrelevant, while perhaps funny, only distracts. Oftentimes someone will describe a very funny commercial, but when asked, he or she is unable to say who the advertiser was.

Lastly, an individual who is enthusiastic, positive, and upbeat will have a much better chance of creating and selling big ideas. Everyone—agency, client, and consumers—responds to enthusiasm. Fortunately, while to a certain degree inborn, this is a mentality that can be developed and improved over time.

Agency individuals who seek the kinds of knowledge described, people who have the attitudes and mentalities mentioned, are those who are most likely to be the sources of big ideas. Agencies that attract and keep a number of people having these qualities and attitudes will prosper. One big idea, an idea that drives a business ahead, will positively affect the individual or individuals involved and will greatly enhance the agency. The reputation of the agency associated with several big ideas will soar. Doyle, Dane & Bernbach was responsible for the very successful and very visible campaigns for Volkswagen, Avis, and Levy's bread in the 1960s. People are still talking about these ads more than 20 years later, even though the agency no longer exists. More recently, Hill, Holliday, a small, Boston-based agency, vastly increased its creative reputation and subsequently its business volume with a successful campaign for John Hancock. Chiat Day became known and recognized largely for its work on behalf of Nike.

So what's the big idea? The big idea is what the client is seeking and is willing to do anything to find, including replacing the ad agency. It is what agency individuals are after to enhance their careers, and it is what an agency needs in order to prosper. Fortunately, the big idea has been created and, therefore, it can be created again. An agency applying the right mix of science and art, systems and sensitivities, can create the right mix of people and environment for big ideas to be born. The big idea is worth the effort.

CHAPTER 6

CLIENT RELATIONSHIPS

Managing client relationships must be a top agency management priority. Most agency managers tend to think in terms of *maintaining* client relationships for the short term as opposed to *managing* these relationships for growth over the long term. However, like anything else, a management plan and a system for monitoring the plan can reap large rewards. This chapter deals with a variety of means for ensuring that client relationships are strong and continue to improve. First it outlines the possible causes of disruptions in client relationships—the danger signs of more serious rifts. The chapter also encompasses a range of client relationship subjects, including the senior management–client management contact; agency evaluations; client progress reports; managing clients better by educating them to be better clients; and finally, a look at handling difficult clients.

CLIENT RELATIONSHIP PITFALLS

The relationship between an advertising agency and its clients is similar to an individual's relationship with a bank account. An individual with a bank account is wise to build up cash equity in preparation for those occasions when significant withdrawals must be made. Likewise, unless the agency builds up equity for the inevitable problems that will develop in client relationships, it will not be able to overcome these crises. Equity with the client is built up over time by maintaining good relationships at all levels of the client organization, by consistently delivering a quality agency product, and by convincing the client that the agency is a good value, that it is honest, and that it has the client's best interests at heart for the long-term future. Regardless of how well the agency performs, agency-client problems arise for a number of reasons.

One significant reason for client problems is that the client is in a bad business situation. When a company's business suffers—for whatever reason—all of its suppliers and most particularly its advertising agency are in jeopardy of being dragged into that bad situation. The more important advertising is to the success of the client's business, the more likely the agency will receive criticism as a result of the client's bad business situation. In general, the higher the ratio of advertising-to-sales dollars, the more likely advertising will be suspect if sales decline. For example, a whole range of beauty and cosmetic products, especially those in the higher price ranges, have advertising-to-sales ratios of 50 percent, meaning that for every dollar of sales, 50 cents is spent on advertising. Even in areas where advertising is a smaller percentage of sales, if business declines, client management is going to take a hard look at advertising. Most consumer products have advertising-to- sales ratios closer to 10 percent, yet the total dollars involved in advertising can be enormous. (Budgets of $30 million for brands of cigarettes, for example, are not unusual.) The point is, a bad client business situation is a clear warning signal that trouble lies ahead for the advertising agency.

A second and probable cause for a drop in the level of the agency-client relationship is management turnover within the client's organization. Such personnel changes are inevitable. When this happens, a whole new set of dynamics are put into motion, ones with which the agency must deal from the outset. Obviously, the more sweeping the changes, the more likely problems are to develop. It is one thing to see a client product manager change (which is common), but it is more unsettling to see a change in marketing manager, in marketing director or a president, or even in a combination of these positions. A glance at the business section of the morning newspaper demonstrates the amount of change, and the raft of mergers and acquisitions of the 1980s has exacerbated this problem. Client personnel turnover is one of the most frustrating parts of the advertising business because the agency is often forced to start all over again. An educational program, as well as a whole series of events aimed at building respect and rapport for the agency, is needed, and this takes months to effect.

A third and obvious cause of disruption in the agency-client relationship is an agency performance problem, whether real or imagined. Since there rarely is evidence that the advertising is working (i.e., building sales), it is easy for clients to judge that the work is subpar. If the agency changes the key creative people on the client's business, even though it is the correct decision to make, the client may consider this to be mistreatment. It is for this reason that agency-client evaluations, either formal or informal, are a necessity.

Agency performance problems can run the gamut from strategic issues to the advertising itself, to media mistakes, or to a whole host of administrative problems including misbudgeting client monies. If the agency spends twice as much as planned in Topeka and only half as much as planned in Youngstown, and these cities are both test markets for a new product, a very irate client will be calling. These kinds of mistakes put a dent in the relationship with the client, and unless the equity referred to earlier has accumulated, it is sometimes hard to overcome the problems.

With the actual advertising, most often the cause of agency-client breakdowns is either a disagreement about or a misunderstanding of the advertising strategy for the brand or service. This is why it is paramount that an agency has a strategic system that both the agency and client believe in and practice, one that the agency has convinced the client is both valid and valuable. Agencies inevitably encounter problems with creative executions, and unless the client believes in the strategy, these problems can lead to upheaval.

The chemistry between the agency and the client is something that must be constantly monitored by agency management. This, too, can be measured in part by periodic agency evaluations. The chemistry is important at all levels, and breakdown at any given level can lead to discontent and disruption. The agency-client chemistry equation at the highest levels, however, is the most difficult to measure. Too often, agency top management is unrealistic about agency-client relationships at these high levels. Many times it is assumed that a given agency executive has excellent relationships with his or her client counterparts, although this may not be true. The agency executive vice-president in charge of the account is supposed to be a close friend of the client president, but may not be. Nor is it uncommon for the agency individual to be unaware that his or her relationship has soured, or to be reluctant to tell peers of a worsening situation. Therefore, cross-checks at the highest levels are in order. An agency contact grid sheet should be prepared for each client and should be monitored quarterly.

Conflicts, of course, can affect client relationships. Conflicts occur when agencies are found to be in violation of client conflict policies, which, in general, are aimed at preventing an agency from working for a competing client or product. Usually, the policy is quite clear. Procter & Gamble, for example, expects that the agency assigned to its detergent business will not take a similar assignment from a competing soap manufacturer.

Other conflict policies and attitudes are less defined. A notable account change involving a massive switch of billings occurred in 1988, when RJR, which had only a few years before merged with Nabisco, fired Dancer Fitzgerald because the agency (a cookie, not a tobacco agency) had run an antismoking commercial for another client, Northwest Airlines. Over $100 million in billings were moved. This case demonstrates the emotional element of conflicts. Too often the blame for a conflict is placed on the client's doorstep. The truth is, if agencies are willing to plan ahead, they can avoid conflict and enhance client relationships.

The agency needs a comprehensive growth plan to accomplish these goals. It must select product and service categories and clients it wants to grow with over the long term. Determining the best long-term and geographic alignments, category by category, must be an agency practice that is updated annually. A wise agency will make a long-term commitment to a client in a given category if the client will honor this commitment and assign the agency either an existing or a new product in this category at the agency if the opportunity arises. Obviously, this decision must be made carefully as it certainly is not wise for an agency to stay out of a category for an extended period of time in the hope that a client will reward it. If an agency, in an attempt to secure an assignment, tells a fast-food client that it will stay out of the fast-food business, and several years pass without an assignment, the agency perhaps has lost out on millions of fast-food billings from other clients. On the other hand, an agency must avoid the propensity to take assignments from clients just to obtain short-term income. Often this results in conflicts that limit long-term growth.

The effects of mergers and acquisitions on agency relationships has taken center stage in recent times. Here, too, an agency can often influence these events with careful, ongoing analysis of client merger/acquisition potential. The agency's new business team should analyze existing clients and top prospects to project how these companies fit together. This analysis can only be made from a marketing standpoint, not from the often controlling financial standpoint. Nevertheless, the analysis is a worthwhile endeavor because the stakes can be large and the rewards great.

An agency's competition can cause problems to develop between the agency and its clients. This is true when a client employs more than one agency. Sometimes, however, the problem is greater when the client uses only one agency. This agency has much more to lose when the client is tempted to talk to new agencies to look for greener grass. On the other hand, such clients as Philip Morris and Lever that employ many agencies can assess the quality not only of the individual agencies, but of the industry overall. Therefore, in single-agency situations, agency management must be more alert to the development of problems.

A major cause for a breakdown in the agency-client relationship is a problem with the compensation system used by the client and/or the lack of account profitability. Of course, the compensation system and account profitability are inextricably linked. However, it does not always follow that the higher the effective commission rate, the higher the profitability. (Effective rate is mathematically derived by dividing total agency income, whether from commission or fees, by client billings.) In fact, agencies have lost money on 15 percent commission accounts and made money on 10 percent accounts. The single largest determinant of agency profitability is the size of the account, not the compensation system in use. Generally, the bigger the account, the greater the profitability. So while it follows that the bigger the account and the higher the commission rate, the more money the agency should make, the simple truth is the agency has very little control over either billings or billing rates.What the agency can do—in fact, must do—to achieve respectable profitability levels is to develop compensation systems tailored to the individual needs of its clients. For example, an agency with 10 clients will have 10 compensation arrangements.

Practically all clients say that it is important for their agency to be profitable on their accounts, and most, in fact, honestly believe this. Therefore, agencies should periodically review profitability problems with clients in an effort to correct them. Agencies, however, are reluctant to do this. Rather, they look to improve profitability by reducing costs. While this action will make the profit-and-loss sheet look better, at the same time it necessarily impairs the agency's performance level in the eyes of the client. This is because the only significant way to reduce agency costs on an account is to reduce the number of people assigned to that account. When this happens, the agency lessens its ability to develop a better compensation system.

It should be the avowed objective of the agency to make all accounts profitable. The agency evaluation, discussed later in the chapter, is an excellent forum for discussing compensation. The client progress report, also discussed later in the chapter, is the means by which the agency becomes knowledgeable about client compensation or profitability problems, as well as other problems.

MANAGEMENT CONTACT

While it is obvious that contact with clients is a paramount management interest, it is an area that is most often mismanaged. Like everything else in the management of an agency, client contact requires a plan derived from collaborative thought, as well as a system for monitoring the progress of the plan. This plan must have some dynamics at work if it is to succeed.

First of all, a client-contact plan must identify the key client individuals to be contacted. Second, it must identify those agency individuals who are going to contact each client individual. Importantly, it must include overlap of agency people calling on any given client, for no client management individual should be called upon by just one agency manager. This rule, more than any other, is violated by agencies, and the pitfalls of this violation are many. First of all, the agency's assumption that the agency individual has a good relationship with the client can be incorrect: for example, the agency individual assumes he or she has a good relationship when often he or she does not; a senior agency individual misleads agency counterparts into believing that he or she has an excellent relationship with a client even though the individual knows this is not true; or an agency vice-president pretends that he or she has a close association with the client marketing director. Therefore, it is important that each key client has a relationship with at least two senior agency individuals so that he or she has a feel for the total agency, not just one individual's representation of it. Logically, the more members of agency management a client knows, the more comfortable that client becomes with the entire agency and its efforts.

Exhibit 6–1 shows a hypothetical matrix grid that can be used to monitor the frequency of agency-client contact. A member of the operations committee should be responsible for keeping tabs on these contacts and for reporting their progress at quarterly update meetings. There is no question that if left to chance, which is the way most agencies approach senior management contact responsibilities, the agency will lose meaningful contact with the client. This will only work against the agency over the long haul.

EXHIBIT 6–1
Hypothetical Client Contact Grid

Client Individuals	Cartwright Chair, CEO	Harris President, COO	Watkins EVP-Client Services	Burns, EVP	Olsen, EVP	Murphy Senior VP
Smith, Chair, CEO	2	2				1
Jones, President COO	2	2				1
Smithers, President, International	1	4	2	1		
Wilkens, EVP, Consumer Products	1	3	6	2		3
Corington, Senior VP, Director Marketing		2	8	4		4
Spence, Senior VP, Advertising Services		2	2		3	6
O'Brien, Senior VP, Marketing Division A		2		2		12
Shapiro, Senior VP, Marketing Division B		2		2	2	11

Client Name:
Agency Individuals

AGENCY EVALUATIONS

While the image of the advertising business is one of complaining clients, the opposite is really true. It is human nature to be reluctant to criticize. Clients often hide their concerns and perhaps subjugate them over time until it is critical or too late for the agency to respond to the problem. Perhaps, for example, a number of client people feel uncomfortable with the senior agency individual assigned to their business, but the problem is not severe enough on any given day to warrant a complaint. Then, one day, a problem develops over a particular commercial, and all the latent animosity toward the agency erupts. To clear the air and to provide the agency with meaningful information on where it stands with a client, periodic agency evaluations are a must. While an annual evaluation will suffice, semi-annual evaluations are ideal. The purpose of these evaluations is to have key agency and client individuals candidly discuss their relationships. Although rare, the ideal conversation will provide an opportunity for the agency to discuss the attributes and shortcomings of the client's organization and to discuss the client's approach to the advertising process.

While many clients have elaborate processes for evaluating agencies, these need not be so complicated. Exhibit 6–2 is a simplified version of an agency evaluation form, which provides the opportunity for key comments on those factors that are critical to the agency's performance. When all is said and done, the real purpose of the evaluation process is to get the key people in a room so they can talk openly about their relationships. Whatever form or forum is used to make this happen is a good one.

Once a year, agency management should examine the client list to determine which clients are providing evaluations and which are not. In order to achieve the goal of 100 percent feedback, management must be assertive with both the clients and those agency employees responsible for handling the evaluation.

CURRENT CLIENT PROGRESS REPORT

Exhibit 6–3 shows a prototypical current client progress report. It is suggested that this report be filled out semiannually by the management supervisor or key account management individual responsible for a given client. This report is intended to give management a fast and timely update of the client's business condition. It can be used by management as a planning tool and is also helpful as background material for top client management contacts.

The first section deals with client information. It includes a list of key client individuals by title and, importantly, a parallel list of agency personnel who are responsible for primary contact with each of the client individuals. Obviously, this must be

EXHIBIT 6–2
Advertising Agency Evaluation Form

Agency Name:
Date of Review:
Date of Last Review:

For each dimension below, rate the agency as excellent, good, fair, or poor.

Creative

Strategic direction and participation
Idea generation
Campaign generation
Production capabilities
Backup creativity
Overall contribution

Research

Idea generation/innovation
Analytical abilities
Research capabilities
Overall contribution

Media

Idea generation/innovation
Planning
Buying
Monitoring, accountability
Overall contribution

Account Management

Participation, innovation in business-building ideas
Strategic direction
Leadership of the product group

Agency Overall

Quality of agency involvement in business-building ideas and strategic
    development
Quality of agency product
Overall level of agency product group
Agency top management involvement
Management and control of client monies
Continuity of people assigned to the business

EXHIBIT 6–3
Current Client Progress Report

Client Name:

---

1. List key client individuals, including titles. Indicate agency individual with primary responsibility for each client contact.
2. Briefly describe overall state of client's business and of each agency assignment.
3. Describe current state of agency relationship. Use specific client comments, and summarize any informal or formal agency evaluations.
4. Financial data: Provide three-year summary of billings, income, expenses, and profits.
5. Provide information related to growth possibilities for this client. What billings growth can be anticipated for current agency assignments? What new product or other brand assignments could the agency handle, and what are the prospects for these? Are there any other allied services the agency could be providing for this client?
6. Potential problems can develop if one or more of the following situations exist. Please check those that you consider to be current or imminent problems.
   _____Client business problem.
   _____Client managerial change.
   _____Agency performance problem.
   _____Conflict problems.
   _____Merger/acquisition problems.
   _____Compensation/profitability problems.
   _____Competing agency problems.

---

updated regularly. This is a brief summary of information contained in the client contact grid shown in Exhibit 6–1.

A brief description of the client's overall business and particularly of the state of the client's business as it affects the agency assignment follows. This is an important part of the report.

The report also includes a brief description of the agency's relationship with the client. This should be as specific as possible and should include some definitive information from the client gained either from a client evaluation or an informational meeting with top management. As noted earlier, where a client review procedure does not exist, it is in the agency's best interest to insist upon the implementation of one.

The next section of the client progress report should show three-year results of agency billings, income, expenses, and profits. This section is followed by a description of the growth possibilities for the agency. This subject is most important to management as it provides information about the client's growth direction. Any business-building efforts that are underway, any new product or line extensions that may be under consideration, and possible uses of additional agency resources for a client's business should be pointed out here.

Finally, the report lists the problems that may have developed between client and agency, problems that were described at the beginning of this chapter. It is critical that agency management is aware of any problems that exist.

The current client progress report is an important management tool that should be implemented regularly. This report should be used as a basis for discussion within the agency, as well as between client and agency management.

MANAGING THE CLIENT

For the same agency cost, one client can get brilliant advertising while a second receives mediocre or worse advertising. Usually, though, the best clients get the best advertising. Although an agency's management often thinks about managing the agency, it rarely thinks about managing its clients. However, it *is* possible to manage the client; the client then becomes a better client and therefore gets better and more advertising impact for the dollar. There are a number of areas within the client's organization that can be improved. This improvement will allow for better agency-client relationships and, eventually, for better advertising.

One good example of an area for improvement is client structure, that is, the organizational setup with which the client deals with the agency. Too many client levels are the enemy of good ideas, just as too many levels within the agency itself are counterproductive. Therefore, the agency should analyze client structure for opportunities to recommend simplified structures for dealing with the advertising. Without a doubt, the clients receiving the best advertising have only a few (two or three) levels dealing with the advertising the agency prepares. This does not mean that the client does not have more structural levels for marketing needs. Rather, it suggests that these levels collapse when it comes to dealing with advertising. This reduction in levels is accomplished when the client insists on only two or three approval levels within the company and informs the agency of such a system. Another way to reduce levels is to bring client top management into the decision-making process early. Numerable meetings on an advertising strategy at lower, nondecision-making levels, when top management is on another track, are one cause of decreased agency profitability and productivity.

Part and parcel of the preceding discussion is identification of the client individual who has final responsibility for advertising approval. While on paper this might seem obvious, in practice it often is not. Sometimes people with titles that sound like they are responsible for advertising do not really have that responsibility. Therefore, in a fuzzy situation, the agency should press the client into clearly stating who has responsibility for advertising approval and into identifying the channels of authority. For example, it could be clearly stated that the director of marketing has final say on advertising matters. The director of marketing, in turn, could state that all those beneath him or her will meet as a group to review advertising and that the second in command, the marketing manager, will manage these meetings and will be in charge. In such a situation, the agency knows it is dealing basically with only two client levels in the decision process.

Advertising is adversely affected by a failure at the strategic level. This can take many forms. Often a strategy is not written clearly enough so that both the agency and the client understand the purpose of the advertising. Even when clearly written, misinterpretation is possible. Months and sometimes years of effort are wasted because there is not complete agreement on strategic focus. Agencies should insist, if necessary, on off-campus meetings with key clients to thrash out the meaning of the strategy before advertising development begins.

Another way that an agency can manage a client is to analyze the client's use of research and to recommend to the client the best use of research, both market and copy. Blind acceptance of copy research systems over the years has resulted in a great deal of safe, but mediocre, advertising. Agencies complain about research, but often do not attempt to educate their clients of its true role. The emphasis should be on research's role in setting strategy and on its role as a diagnostic aid in the development of copy, as opposed to its traditional role as a reward or punishment mechanism at the end of the advertising process.

Agencies can also improve their clients' approach to advertising by insisting that the clients focus on their real needs. Too often, priorities get lost, and a great deal of agency work is devoted to alternative strategies, alternative campaigns, and backup campaigns. Often, these alternatives and backups never see the light of day because when they are most needed, the marketing environment has changed from the time that they were created. All of this extra work drains agencies and dilutes their focuses on the high priority current needs of their clients. Periodic reviews with top client management of all the work in process help relieve this problem. For example, a coffee manufacturer asks the advertising agency to develop an alternative campaign based on assumed economies in coffee consumption during the next year that are anticipated because of price declines in Brazil. The agency completes the work, but coffee prices rise instead. The campaign is of no use. The client could have better used the agency's energies on a campaign that had a greater chance of exposure and was not subject to the vicissitudes of a foreign country. While the client may think that the agency has an unending reservoir of talent to devote to business, this is not so, even in the largest client situations. Moreover, agency people become cynical, frustrated, and seek other agency assignments when they perceive they are working on campaigns that will never reach fruition.

Agencies should encourage clients to respond more quickly to ideas. When clients bend over backwards to be polite and are fearful of hurting agency relationships or creative people's feelings, ideas often drag on, usually to the detriment of these ideas. Clients should be urged to reject bad ideas quickly.

Agencies can improve their clients' ability to manage the advertising process by urging them to provide rewards for jobs well done, either individually or by the collective agency. These need not be monetary, although such rewards can be a great incentive. Other motivators are such recognition devices as the

President's Award or the Advertisement of the Year Award. It is remarkable how much power a slight nod of approval from a client has over agency individuals, particularly creative ones. It is also remarkable that hardly any clients recognize these simple, inexpensive methods for motivating their agencies.

As stated earlier in this chapter, formal evaluations of the agency by clients are essential to good agency relationships. Nowhere is this more important than in the area of advertising development. Agencies should examine their client lists, if some clients are not providing evaluations, they should be asked to conduct them.

Another way to manage the client and to improve relationships is to insist upon financial openness. Annual reviews of agency profitability can be very constructive. Smart clients want their agencies to be rewarded for their efforts. These clients recognize the value of incentives, as well. Therefore, it makes sense for candor to pervade agency-client discussions of finances.

Another way that an agency can encourage its clients to be better managers of the advertising process is to urge them to make the process fun. Agency people are attracted to those client individuals who are open and fair and with whom it is fun to do business. This does not suggest throwing parties; rather, it means providing an atmosphere that makes agencies want to work with their clients. This is a highly subjective, amorphous area, but one that will bear much fruit if practiced well. For example, client management can set a tone of openness by treating the agency as a business partner, not just a supplier of a service. This means providing confidential data to help in the formulation of strategy, treating agency individuals respectfully during meetings, correspondence, and day-to-day activities, and sincerely trying to develop personal relationships with agency people outside normal business activities.

GETTING ALONG WITH DIFFICULT CLIENTS

It is guaranteed that any agency roster includes a few difficult clients. Whether or not the client organization itself is difficult, there are always some individuals with whom it is difficult to deal. This is integral to the advertising business. Fortunately, there are ways to deal with difficult client organizations, as well as with difficult client employees. None of these ways is guaranteed to work, but all are worth pursuing since there is nothing more demoralizing to an agency than a particularly difficult client organization and/or client individual.

There are a variety of reasons a client organization is difficult to manage from an advertising agency's standpoint. One reason might be the history and culture of the client company. Perhaps the founder of the company treated agencies in a derisive and menial fashion, and subsequent managements have continued to adopt this tone. A second reason could be the nature of the client's business and the importance of the advertising. For example, advertising might be perceived as only a small factor of the marketing mix so the client treats it accordingly. Another reason could be that the client organization is so bureaucratic that it is almost impossible to get advertising approved. Perhaps there are six levels of approval within the organization, as well as a rigid copy research system that is difficult to follow. Another difficult client may simply have a history of changing agencies. If the client has changed agencies every 2 years for the past 10 years, then chances are that the client will not maintain a working relationship with an agency. A final and sure way to become a difficult client is to underpay the agency so that the agency is constantly looking for ways to make money on the account. For example, if a client decides to pay the agency 12 percent commission, despite the fact that the standard practice is 14 percent for the particular product category, the agency must cut corners to make the account profitable.

The truth is, however, difficult clients can be handled if the agency has analyzed the situation well enough to know the cause of the problem. If, for example, the problem is a function of the processes that the client employs in the development of the marketing and advertising plans, then the agency certainly can address these processes by informing the client of the frailties in the system and contrasting the client's system with those with more positive results. For example, a client has several marketing, advertising strategy, and advertising execution documents that must be formulated and agreed upon before any creative work can be initiated. The client and agency, as a result, are trapped in a quagmire of paper, and no advertising is completed. Since most, if not all, clients are ready to listen to an agency's opinion or process-related issues, this situation can be changed.

If the way the client organization is structured is at the heart of the difficulty, here, too, a reasonable agency approach is to suggest to the client alternative structures, including the benefits and drawbacks of each as learned from agency experience. An agency can demonstrate that the fewer the levels of advertising approval, the better the advertising.

If the client problem stems from compensation, the agency should alert the client to the problem by showing alternative compensation that is more beneficial to both. For example, if the client is compensating the agency on a 15 percent commission basis, but the billings are too low to cover agency costs, an alternative fee-based system could provide both parties with a workable, long-term method of doing business.

If the difficulty in the client relationship is top client management's deep-rooted philosophy, culture, and/or point of view, the agency may find it more difficult to effect changes. However, here, too, a reasonable approach by the agency often can make a difference.

Dealing with a difficult client individual is a different situation altogether. Difficult individuals obviously can show up in the best of client organizations, although they are more likely to be part of a difficult organization. One effective way to solve a difficult client situation is to find the person within the agency who is most capable of dealing with the difficult individual. This may take a lot of trial and error, but in most agency situations, casting is key. Sometimes a complete restaffing of the agency product group is necessary. The inherent risk of doing this, however, is losing the history and understanding of the account that has accumulated over time. Therefore, selective restructuring, rather than total restructuring, of the agency staff is more likely to be successful.

In particularly difficult client situations, confrontation with the individual sometimes works. Another solution may be reporting the deterioration of the relationship to the individual's superior. However, this approach is seldom successful. The individual client has gained responsibility because the client organization management thinks highly of him or her, and management is unlikely to remove the individual just because of agency difficulties. Moreover, it is likely that the individual will learn of the agency's report and will become even more difficult. Attacking an individual client by going above him or her is a last-resort tactic.

Of course, the proven way for dealing with a difficult client individual is to outlast him or her. One way to do this is to rotate agency personnel on the account with the agreement that time on the business will be of a certain duration. Knowing that the assignment has an ending makes it easier to endure.

When all else fails and the frustration levels are high, the ultimate way to deal with a difficult client organization is to terminate the business relationship. Agencies are rightfully reluctant to give up income, but sometimes resigning the business is the most therapeutic way to deal with the situation. If the difficulty with the client is well-known throughout the client organization, perhaps even the industry, then agency pride and dignity are preserved through resignation. A great boost in morale can occur, and this can pay important future dividends, though immeasurable, to the agency. Sometimes it allows the agency to attract a better client in the same category. Young & Rubicam, for example, resigned the entire Gallo wine account, much to the delight of agency personnel. Soon after, the agency was able to win the Inglenook wine account, a relationship that has been rewarding for both sides for 10 years.

CASE HISTORY

An instructive agency-client relationship is Young & Rubicam (Y&R)–Procter & Gamble (P&G), which, unfortunately, ended in divorce even though each company was, and is, respected in its field as one of the best, if not the very best. The case demonstrates that despite talent, good intentions, and integrity, mistakes can be made and long-term relationships can be impaired and even severed. In this particular case, the relationship lasted decades, from the 1950s to the 1980s.

The heart of the disagreement between the two companies was P&G's clearly defined and restrictive conflict policy, which stated that if an agency had an assignment from one of its six divisions, that agency could not take on a brand deemed competitive to *any* other brand within that division. The policy presented no problem to most divisions because of their singular nature. The bar soap and household cleaner division, the packaged soap and detergent division, the coffee division, and the paper division made and marketed products under these descriptions. The foods division and the toiletries division, while in the businesses their names imply, actually were involved in a wide variety of product categories. Toiletries, for example, encompassed deodorants, toothpastes, shampoos, and a host of toiletry-related products. If a P&G agency was assigned any one brand from the toiletries division, for example, that agency could not take a toiletry product from any other manufacturer. While restrictive, such a policy was not necessarily a problem to most P&G agencies since P&G brands were leaders, billings were large, and once understood, the P&G system could be profitable. Also, P&G management and employees were generally of the highest caliber, both professionally and as human beings.

The situation with Y&R was unique. Because of its size (number one in the United States) and its 60-year history, Y&R had developed lengthy and sizeable relationships with many leading packaged goods companies. According to the P&G policy, Y&R could work only with the two soap divisions, having conflicts to one degree or another with the other four. Further, the Y&R assignments from P&G were limited—only one brand from each division. Therefore, Y&R billings in the United States from P&G were small (under $20 million).

Several other factors were important. First, Y&R was a leading agency for P&G outside the United States. P&G's major overseas categories were soaps and detergents, and Y&R had a number of leading brands in many key overseas markets. Second, Y&R had an image problem in the United States as far as P&G's management was concerned that dated back to the 1960s, when current P&G top management was in the lower and middle ranks. The perceived image, which was outdated, was that Y&R was nonstrategic, executionally oriented almost to an experimental degree, and, therefore, not to P&G's liking.

Remarkable as it seems, 20 years later members of P&G management could remember a Y&R general presentation to P&G's marketing corps that struck them as outlandish, irrelevant, and insulting, they could even recall details of that presentation. Because Y&R had such a small U.S. assignment base, however, there were limited opportunities to reverse this poor image through excellent performance.

Adding to the overall problem was the fact that in any given year, Y&R lost money on U.S. P&G business. They did, however, make money on overseas business.

Despite all these complications, Y&R vowed to become a bigger and more significant agency to P&G in the United States. This was accomplished by assigning the very best people to the P&G business and by total involvement by Y&R management in the P&G business, both in the United States and overseas.

For a period of time, the strategy worked for Y&R. P&G responded positively to the agency's increased efforts, and after several years of improved performance, P&G rewarded the agency. It assigned a new product to the agency, and soon after, a second new product. Each product was from one of the two divisions currently working with the agency. From P&G's standpoint, it was an extremely positive sign of renewed faith in the agency. From the agency's standpoint, it was also recognized as an accomplishment because P&G took new product assignments seriously and because of the sizeable billings potential of a new product (first-year national billings in the $25–$50 million range).

There were two problems with the assignments, however. First, even the best new products—ones that do exceptionally well in test markets—take several years to reach national status. During such time, the agency could expect to sustain the expenses of an ongoing brand of up to a million dollars per year per brand. Second, P&G's policy called for a small annual agency remuneration in the area of $50,000. P&G was accustomed to assigning new products to agencies that normally had significant existing P&G income and profit so that the new product work could be absorbed until the new brand became profitable. This approach was similar to that of other major packaged goods manufacturers—client and agency alike shared in the risks and rewards of new product marketing. Unfortunately, this policy only makes sense if there are large existing bases of business between the two parties. As noted, Y&R was already losing money in the United States on the P&G business.

Several developments in the 1980s exacerbated the situation. First, for a variety of reasons, the agency's P&G business overseas went from a significant profit to a significant loss. Second, both of the new brands encountered stumbling blocks. In each case, the problems were not unreasonable, but they were time consuming. Finally, Y&R accepted a brand assignment from the Gillette Company for Right Guard® deodorant.

As a result of Y&R's actions, P&G fired the agency in the United States, the Gillette assignment apparently flying in the face of some future assignment P&G planned for the agency, although nothing of this was ever officially stated. P&G management may have believed that this new Y&R-Gillette assignment reduced the possibility for long-term growth. It was rumored at the time that P&G would divide its toiletries division, thereby reducing existing conflict problems for its agencies, including Y&R.

The remarkable fact about the dismissal of Y&R in the United States is that it inevitably meant that the entire global relationship was for all intents and purposes over. Global marketing is an old phenomenon to some brands, the Coca-Cola–McCann-Erickson relationship being a prime example. Certainly, in the early 1980s both P&G and Y&R were aware of the trend toward global marketing and the increasing practice of assigning a product to an agency on a worldwide basis. Therefore, it was difficult to imagine Y&R and P&G continuing in a relationship that excluded the most profitable part of the world, the United States.

Within a year of Y&R's losing the U. S. portion of the P&G business, the agency resigned the P&G overseas business and announced a major $100 million$^+$ association with Colgate.

What conclusions can be drawn from this case in the context of agency-client relationships? First, despite the long-term relationship between the two companies, there was not clear communication of the needs of either. If P&G had reevaluated Y&R and had decided to reward its efforts, new product assignments were not the answer. The costs of new product work could only make the economic situation worse for the agency. If P&G wanted the agency to be a long-term partner, it should have set the economics straight in some fashion.

Second, neither company seemed to understand the globalism of the issue. Each company should have asked, Do I want to be a worldwide partner with this company? If P&G had asked that question, it most assuredly would have answered yes since Y&R already had a large share of its overseas business. Moreover, Y&R had great potential in the United States, where it was acknowledged as one of the two or three best agencies, as well as the largest. If P&G was thinking of changing its divisional arrangement or altering its policy, it could have discussed this with the agency. Ironically, for all its thoroughness and systems, P&G did not share agency evaluations with its agencies. Although the agency had made known its economic problems to P&G and P&G had been sympathetic and even tried to help, the agency continued to lose money. No agency-client relationship, regardless of size, can survive if the agency does not make a profit. If Y&R was not prospering in the United States, the entire relationship was unsound. To stabilize the relationship, P&G could have rewarded Y&R with an ongoing brand with ongoing income, instead of with new products.

Y&R had not discussed the possibility of accepting the Gillette assignment with P&G. This was an error in judgment because the situation would have come to a head.

As a result of these events, both companies were losers. P&G lost a valuable worldwide resource. They also had to go through the inevitable problems associated with agency switches, a process that takes 6 to 12 months. Y&R, while gaining Colgate, lost as a client what at the time was the biggest advertiser. On both sides, some professional and personal friendships that had been decades in the making were lost.

The case demonstrates the intricacies of agency-client relationships. It also emphasizes the need to constantly communicate, particularly at the highest levels.

CHAPTER 7

AGENCY GROWTH

PERSPECTIVE ON GROWTH

In all business enterprises, without growth there is the likelihood of stagnation and subsequent decline. To be vital and successful an agency must grow. The best agencies grow at an average rate of over 10 percent per year. Historically, the very best agencies have done better than this even during the recessionary years. One beneficial factor, particularly in the United States, is that media inflation tends to be greater than general inflation as measured by the consumer price index (C.P.I.). Therefore, clients have raised budgets faster than agencies have had to raise expenses, resulting in higher profit levels. This phenomenon was more helpful to agencies during the early half of the 1980s rather than during the latter half of this decade when the C.P.I. has been rising at a 4 to 5 percent rate and media inflation at a 6 to 8 percent rate. Part of the reason for media inflation dropping from a double-digit rate (more than 10 percent) in the early part of the 1980s is the increasing competition between network TV and cable TV, which has had a negative effect on network TV pricing.

Another external factor, particularly affecting American-based international agencies, has been the value of the dollar compared to major market currencies in Europe and Japan. Here, too, the first half of the 1980s is in contrast to the second half. As the dollar increased in relative value during the early 1980s, advertisers in the United Kingdom, Germany, Italy, France, and Japan, while perhaps increasing budgets in their own currencies, after translation actually generated the same or fewer dollars than in previous years. Beginning in early 1985, the reverse was true, with the dollar falling rapidly against foreign money, thereby generating higher dollar budgets for American agencies operating in those countries.

In Latin America, exceedingly high rates of inflation have eroded the budgets of American agencies. If these rates continue, as is likely, Latin America will become relatively unimportant to all American companies, including agencies.

Inflation factors and currency translations, while very important to agency growth, are not within the control of agencies. As such, agency management must allow for the effects of these factors, particularly by being conservative when making planning assumptions.

There are three areas of growth available to agencies that are within their control. An agency can grow through merger and acquisition, from greater business from its existing clients, or by attracting totally new clients. All three are essential to the vitality of the agency. This chapter deals with the first two sources. The third source, new business, is so critical to an agency that the next chapter is devoted totally to it.

GROWTH FROM EXISTING CLIENTS

An agency must experience growth from its existing client base if it expects to remain vital. Yet, an agency's existing-client economic base can erode for a variety of reasons. Lost accounts, declining or maturing brands, client profitability problems, lack of confidence in the agency's creative product, and reduced compensation arrangements are just some of the factors that can result in diminished advertising budgets. For example, if several clients reduce commissions, the agency can almost be sure that its income will decline over time. If a client's management determines that promotion dollars are more effectively used in generating sales than is advertising, they are likely to spend less on advertising. An agency that stands by and observes these events without counteractions will have a serious problem on its hands, barring extraordinary new business gains or acquisitions.

Every existing client represents a business opportunity for the agency. Agencies must be proactive, not reactive, to client needs. As noted throughout this book, money chases ideas. Clients will spend behind a good idea, even if there was no budget for the idea before it emerged. Once clients observe that an idea is building business, they will support that idea with more advertising dollars. Therefore, agencies must seek ways to expend their current client bases by developing unsolicited business-building ideas.

A helpful management tool for monitoring and effecting this attitude is shown in Exhibit 7–1, the current client growth report. This report should be updated twice a year by the agency personnel closest to the client situation. It also should be presented to management so that it has a clear understanding of each account's growth possibilities. This report, along with the current

EXHIBIT 7–1
Current Client Growth Report

Client Name:

This report includes all agency efforts to foster the growth of the client's business.

1. *Growth from the use of other agency services.* Identify additional agency services (e.g., sales promotion, direct mail, yellow pages, public relations) that could be provided to this client. Describe specific actions to accomplish this. Indicate annual income potential.
2. *Growth from new products.* Describe the client's new product program. Identify new product possibilities for the agency, as well as the specific actions for obtaining assignments. Indicate income potential.
3. *Growth from additional office assignments.* Identify client's assignments to other agencies in markets that the agency also services. Describe client's current relationship with other agencies in these markets and agency's prospects for business. Outline steps to obtain account, and estimate income potential.
4. *Growth from business-building ideas.* Outline specific steps the agency is taking to provide this client with unsolicited business-building ideas. Describe next steps, and indicate the income potential.
5. *Overall growth prospects.* Briefly summarize the overall possibilities for growth from this client's business. Indicate the specific actions agency management should undertake.

---

client progress report described in Chapter 6, gives agency management a complete picture of the health of each of its clients.

The report includes four key growth sources: additional agency services, new products, additional office assignments, and business-building ideas. These reports can keep an agency focused on the best income possibilities from existing clients and help in prioritizing agency clients in terms of growth potential.

MERGERS AND ACQUISITIONS

Because an advertising agency's only reason for being is to provide client services at a profit, any merger or acquisition should result in improved service to the agency's clients. The possible improvements in service resulting from merger or acquisition can be grouped into five categories: horizontal growth, vertical growth, geographical growth, people, and fiscal growth. No acquisition should be pursued unless it is absolutely clear that the acquisition candidate will help the agency on at least one of these dimensions.

Horizontal Growth

A horizontal acquisition or diversification offers a consumer agency an allied, relevant communication expertise that can be utilized by the agency's existing clients. Typical examples of this expertise are direct marketing, medical, public relations, and sales promotion. Most of the big agencies have pursued this diversification vigorously in the last decade. Young & Rubicam (Y&R) was the pioneer in this area; it acquired the leading direct marketing company (Wunderman, Ricotta & Kline), the biggest public relations firm (Burson-Marsteller), and the leading medical agency (Sudler & Hennessey), along with some smaller sales promotion, design, and yellow page companies. Most of the other big agencies have followed Y&R's example.

While most agencies now boast of having an array of horizontal communication capabilities, few examples of truly integrated communication programs exist. The reasons for this are discussed in Chapter 10.

Vertical Growth

Vertical integration in an advertising agency can result from mergers and/or acquisitions or even the start-up of agency services or functions that are in line with the agency development process itself. Examples of vertical growth include production facilities, whether in TV or print, program development of media, and outright ownership of media. Agencies have been reluctant to enter into these types of services in large part because of potential client conflicts. The ownership of TV and print production facilities might be considered a conflict of interest, particularly if agencies try to sell these services to current clients. Experiments with such ownership by and large have been unsuccessful. For example, both J. Walter Thompson and Grey have withdrawn from the TV syndication business. Agency ownership of media also could result in a conflict of interest with a client. For example, if an agency owns TV or radio stations, clients would be suspicious of media advertising plans that recommend these properties. An exception is Leo Burnett's reported ownership of an outdoor advertising company.

It is unlikely that vertical integration will be a lucrative area for agency acquisition activities in the near future.

Geographical Growth

Mergers and acquisitions leading to a stronger geographical agency network can be beneficial, particularly to those clients seeking agency network advantages. Besides providing a stronger network, a merger or acquisition can also provide an agency with a facility in a strong geographical market where it previously was not represented. Another important, though more subtle, benefit of geographical growth is a better balance between network or multinational clients and local clients. An agency operation dominated by multinational accounts that are controlled by a home office will not necessarily be a strong operation in its own right. Similarly, an agency that is totally dominated by local accounts will suffer from this imbalance. Therefore, an agency should make acquisitions that will balance its total accounts. The ideal, of course, is 50 percent multinational accounts and 50 percent local accounts. Interpublic achieved this balance in 1988 by acquiring the number one and number two privately owned agencies in Canada. Interpublic then merged these acquisitions with its existing agencies, Lintas and McCann-Erickson.

People

Sometimes an agency merger or acquisition is practical because it provides the merged entity with a greater population of either management or senior specialists in the four key functions: management, creative, media, and account management. Importantly, it can enhance the company's reputation within the industry, which makes the organization more attractive to current employees and to prospective employees. The merger of Ogilvy and Scali, McCabe had this positive effect, even though the two were virtually autonomous. Both agencies had earned strong creative reputations independently; when merged, their combined reputation was even better. The opposite can and has happened; a merged company proves to be less desirable. In this case, the agency not only fails to attract new talent, it also loses its own key talent. The Ally Gargano-MCA merger had this outcome. Ally Gargano had a strong creative image, while MCA had a high management orientation. The combination of cultures, unfortunately, did not gel.

Fiscal Growth

An agency merger or acquisition can and should result in an improved financial situation. If this is not the case, the merger or acquisition can impair the company's ability to serve its clients.

Just as in the marketing of consumer products and services, where the goal is always to improve the consumer's perception of the product or service, any agency merger or acquisition should improve service to the agency's clients. A good way to test this criterion is to list each of the key service functions—account management, creative, media, and research—and to determine as objectively as possible if the merged entity is stronger in each function. If this is not the case, the companies should not be merged.

CHAPTER 8

NEW BUSINESS

PERSPECTIVE ON NEW BUSINESS

Of the three sources of growth available to an agency—growth from existing clients, growth from mergers and acquisitions, and growth from new business—growth from new business is the most important. New business, meaning a totally new brand assignment either from an existing client or from a new client, provides a number of benefits for the agency.

First, of course, new business generates new income, which enables the agency to grow. New business income should be disproportionately profitable, particularly if the agency is careful to slowly add personnel to handle the new account. Expense growth should lag behind income growth in order to maximize profits. In addition, expense growth should never equal revenue growth because efficiencies of scale should be inherent to revenue growth.

A second new business benefit to the agency is the signal it sends to the external community—to clients and to prospects. The signal says that the agency is strong because it has won additional business. The larger and the more prestigious the new business won, the more positive the signal sent. It is particularly reassuring to existing clients to see that the agency has been selected by another client. If, as is practically always the case, the agency wins new business in a competition with other agencies, the victorious agency benefits from the comparison.

A third benefit of new business acquisition is the positive effect it has on agency employees. New business implies that they are working for a successful, vibrant, and growing organization. It indicates that there will be more career opportunities and more economic rewards for the employees. To the extent that the new business was the result of the agency's creative effort, it is a reaffirmation of the agency's creativity.

It is absolutely essential for management to recognize the acquisition of new business by quickly organizing a celebration. Agency people, particularly those who contributed directly to the acquisition should be rewarded.

An agency that fails to win new business for an extended period of time can expect to experience the opposite effects of those described previously. Not only will the economics be negatively affected, but the outside audiences and the agency's employees may lose faith in the agency's abilities. To avoid these repercussions, agency management must consider new business acquisition the highest priority.

ORGANIZATION OF THE NEW BUSINESS DEPARTMENT

The Role of the Chief Executive Officer

Regardless of whether an agency is large or small, the key to its new business success is directly proportional to the effort the chief executive officer (CEO) devotes to this priority. Both within and outside the agency, the CEO must be the leader and focus of the new business operation.

Inside the agency, the CEO must give the proper amount of attention to new business. Furthermore, a significant portion of his or her own time must be devoted to this critical subject. He or she must be an example to the other members of the agency involved in new business. Only by his or her example will the rest of the agency sense the importance of new business and devote the proper amount of time and interest to the subject. It is mandatory that the CEO consistently direct the new business operations of the agency. Otherwise the efforts of the director of new business (if the agency has such a function) and other executives interested in new business will be less than effective. This is because the majority of agency employees are primarily concerned with the day-to-day conduct of ongoing client activities. Because people tend to devote themselves to current client activities and because many avoid the new business area, the agency's new business activity can be stifled unless the CEO makes it known that the agency's new business operation is critical to the future success of the agency.

Outside the agency, the CEO obviously is the focal point for new business. He or she is the most visible agency representative; he or she also has the most leverage to open doors and to gain access to prospects. What the CEO says, how it is said, and where it is said will greatly affect the overall success of the agency and, ultimately, its ability to attract clients.

The wise CEO has a plan detailing exactly how he or she will devote time to the new business development area. The CEO also creates a plan for leading the new business effort within the agency and a schedule outlining the activities he or she will implement outside the agency.

Participation of Other Top Management

Too often in agencies, the CEO and the head of new business are the only individuals spending a significant amount of time on new business. This should not be true, nor does it need to be true. Properly motivated, the majority of the agency's top management can be effective in the acquisition of new accounts. For this to happen, the CEO must make top management aware on a regular basis that it is part of its responsibility to help obtain new accounts. One very effective way to do this is to assign industry prospect categories to top management. For example, if, in a given agency, there are 20 new business targets, these should be divided, 2 categories for each of the 10 senior executives. One executive might be assigned entertainment and transportation, a second detergents and cosmetics, and a third automobiles and computers. Under this system, each member of top management must report periodically to the rest of top management, including the CEO, his or her progress within the assigned industry. This approach assists the head of new business enormously and provides leverage for new business acquisition that most agencies do not utilize.

Characteristics of the Individual in Charge of New Business

In small agencies, the CEO and the person in charge of new business are the same individual. In larger agencies, it is important to have one individual in charge of new business, in addition to the CEO. Whether the new business head devotes all or only part of his or her time to new business depends on the individual and whether or not the company espouses the philosophy that all executives should devote some time to day-to-day activities; that is, no executives are allowed to become purely staff, because this puts them out of touch with the realities of the business. Under such a system, the head of new business would simultaneously handle one or two current accounts within the agency and new business affairs. Because of the extreme pressure and the enormous amount of uncertainty involved in new business, it is also valuable for the head of new business to work on an account on a day-to-day basis.

In any event, there are certain personal characteristics common to successful new business heads. Most likely, the person who is placed in charge of new business has been one of the most, if not the most, successful managers of an ongoing business. The new business head must have great self-confidence; he or she should also be confident of the agency. He or she should be extremely aggressive and persistent because these characteristics are mandatory in seeking new accounts. He or she must have an inner reserve of strength and an overall attitude of optimism since even the most successful new business operation will sometimes fail in an endeavor. In fact, the more active the new business operation, the more likely failures will accompany successes. It is the percentage of success that counts in new business. Therefore, the frequency with which the agency seeks accounts is extremely important. The head of new business must understand this and must be able to bounce back after a defeat and look forward to the next possible victory because his or her attitude will affect other members of the agency. This individual and the CEO are, therefore, partly responsible for employee optimism and eagerness in acquiring new accounts.

Most importantly, the director of new business must be familiar with the capabilities of the agency and knowledgeable about the people within the agency. Someone relatively new to the agency should not be placed in charge of new business, regardless of his or her capabilities, because the success of a new business operation is partly dependent on matching agency resources to the particular needs of prospects. Successful matching is the result of years of familiarity with the workings of the agency. Similarly, the head of new business must be completely knowledgeable about the strengths and weaknesses of the key agency individuals in order to select the right people for individual new business solicitations. This includes selection of those who might work on the solicitation prior to the presentation, as well as those who will be in the meeting itself. Often these two groups of people are separate.

Experience suggests that approximately two years is an appropriate tenure for the head of new business. After two years, he or she tends to lose momentum and may be set in his or her approach to the subject. Because certain actions work in certain new business solicitations, he or she may be convinced that these are the absolute for any and all new business solicitations. Assigning a new individual to the position will breathe life into the agency's new business efforts. However, it is wise to take advantage of the experience gained by the outgoing new business head while he or she was in the position. An agency can develop over time a core of experienced new business employees who are invaluable to the new business operation.

THE TASK-FORCE APPROACH

When it is apparent that a prospect is willing to listen to an agency, it is time for the agency to devote real time and effort to acquisition of this account. The best plan of action is to assign a task force to the account. The task force, which works directly with the head of new business, should comprise key individuals from creative, account management, media, research, and, in certain cases, other specialized areas, such as sales promotion or public relations. These key individuals should be highly experienced and motivated and, if possible, familiar with new business solicitation from earlier task-group experiences. Whether they become the group actually making the presentation or the team proposed to the prospect depends on a variety of factors. Ideally, they will form the group proposed to the prospect, as well as the group making the final presentation. However, remember that the emphasis at this stage of solicitation is on analyzing the client's business. Therefore, the people who work on the task force in the early analytical stages may not necessarily be those who are best for the particular prospect's ongoing needs. Further, presentation skills often are the determinant of who attends the presentation. Ideally, the agency will have trained a variety of people in sound marketing and advertising, as well as in effective presentation.

The task-force approach enables the agency to focus all of its disciplines on a potential client's problems.

HOW MUCH TO BUDGET

Obviously, the amount spent on new business will vary considerably, depending on the size of the agency. Small agencies must devote proportionately more time and effort to new business than must larger agencies.

An agency should spend approximately 2 percent of its revenues on new business efforts, over and above the cost of employee hours logged against the new business. The agency CEO should devote a minimum of 25 percent of his or her time to new business. This percentage is larger for smaller agencies. A director of new business in a smaller agency should expend approximately 50 percent of his or her time on new business; the remaining 50 percent of time should be used for ongoing client handling and other managerial duties.

The amount an agency spends on new business solicitation depends largely on its philosophy concerning presentations that involve speculative creative work. An agency that becomes indiscriminate in seeking accounts through speculative work can go bankrupt from excessive new business costs. The CEO determines when the agency should become involved in speculative work and how much it should spend. This requires extreme care and a realistic estimate of the agency's chances of landing the account.

In many cases, the agency is wise to inform the prospective client of the drawbacks of accepting a speculative campaign. The fact is, most speculative campaigns are unsuccessful because they do not evolve from a thorough understanding of the client's problems.

The most unsophisticated clients are most susceptible to speculative presentations. However, it is these same clients who seem to be continually changing agencies. A successful new business operation should not have to rely a great deal on speculative work.

The 2 percent new business expenditure guideline mentioned previously does not include speculative work. It does include mailings, such as brochures, house advertising, and incidental out-of-pocket costs related to business solicitation.

ADMINISTRATIVE REQUIREMENTS

Whether an agency is large enough to have an administrative new business assistant or not, the administrative requirements are the same. The first requirement is a card for each prospect (see Exhibit 8–1). Obviously, this information should be updated periodically. The cards should be readily accessible to all top executives.

A second requirement is a file for each prospect. Included in this file are all key correspondence between the agency and the prospect, and important reference material related to the client, such as annual reports and articles in business and trade publications.

It is important to house these files in a central agency location. Individual prospect cards and advertising agency and advertiser red books, which are essential reference books, should be stored with these files.

EXHIBIT 8–1
Prospect Information Card

Prospect Name

Primary businesses:
Other businesses:
Businesses of primary interest to the agency:
Billings by category/brand:
Current agency(ies):
Key prospect individuals (name and title):
Description of most recent agency contacts with prospect:
Possible conflict issues:

SELECTING PROSPECTS

After the new business group has been organized and a budget has been established, the next task is to develop the prospect list. The care required to select prospects cannot be overemphasized.

Two factors tend to make most agencies indiscriminate in both their prospect selections and their quests for new accounts. The first is the very real, never-ending need to increase income in the face of constantly rising costs. The second is the desire to demonstrate the agency's vitality through new account acquisitions. These pressures also can lead agencies into the trap of pursuing any and all opportunities, short of obvious conflict situations.

The dangers of this helter-skelter approach are threefold. First, no agency has the resources, either of personnel or funding, to indiscriminately solicit every prospect interested in changing agencies. To the extent that agency employees are diverted from ongoing assignments, this policy will eventually affect the agency's performance on existing accounts.

Second, a shotgun approach most likely will diffuse the focus required for prospects truly representative of worthwhile new business opportunities. The effort required to acquire a quality client is significant. If the agency's new business organization is distracted by too many new business pursuits, it is unlikely that the more lucrative prospects will be sufficiently impressed to switch agencies.

Third, too much new business solicitation, with necessarily limited success, can be demoralizing to the agency's staff. Short of the loss of an account, there is nothing in the advertising business more depressing than losing out on a new business pitch after a great deal of effort and time has been expended. A new business approach that is nonselective can result in poor staff morale and the additional employee turnover inherent to such a situation.

How can an agency avoid these problems? What are the keys to prospect selection? There are a number of steps that can be taken.

THE SIX-STEP PROCESS OF PROSPECT SELECTION

Step 1: Determining the Nonconflict Categories

The first step in developing the prospect list is to determine which industries do not present conflict possibilities. This can be accomplished easily with the help of the industry list provided by the American Association of Advertising Agencies. Even the largest agencies will find there are a number of industries in which they are not represented and that, in theory, are candidates for agency solicitation. Most likely, the list derived from this analysis will be too lengthy and, therefore, unmanageable. This situation leads to step 2 of the process.

Step 2: Prioritizing the Prospect Industries

It is essential that the industries open to the agency are prioritized according to various criteria. This requires careful examination, beginning with determination of absolute size and growth trends for the various prospect industries. Over the years, certain categories have declined in overall size, as well as in the amount of money spent on advertising. Similarly, others show signs of growth. For example, the industries involved in educational and leisure show great promise. Service industries in general are becoming more important than manufacturing companies. The smart agency will spot these areas of growth early and pursue them before their importance is known to all agencies.

In addition to business periodicals and newspapers, other industry research tools exist. Industry and company reports developed by brokerage analysts are excellent and readily available sources of information. The reports issued by the big banks are equally informative.

An honest appraisal of the agency's capabilities, resources, and experiences should factor into prioritizing prospects. It makes no sense to list an industry as a high-priority prospect unless the agency can realistically meet the needs of the companies within that industry.

For example, if the agency and its people have no experience with financial services, the agency will be handicapped in its efforts to acquire a bank, insurance company, or brokerage house. If the agency has no sales promotion arm, it will be at a disadvantage in seeking an airline account.

This analysis requires a keen understanding of the marketing and advertising needs of various industries, plus a cold and objective appraisal of the agency itself. It is essential that this analysis is completed in order to avoid nonproductive account solicitations.

Experience shows that 20 to 25 industry categories is the maximum number of new accounts that a good new business operation can effectively pursue (assuming the agency does at least $40 million in billings). These categories should be divided into high and medium priorities. All other industry prospects, as determined in step 1, are low priorities that should be considered only if a prospect approaches the agency.

Once the high- and medium-priority prospect categories have been selected, the next step is to examine the individual companies within these categories.

Step 3: Determining the Prospect Companies

It does not follow that an agency should consider as prospects all companies within its particular prospect industries. As much care should be devoted to determining the best prospect companies as was expended in determining the best prospect categories.

As with industries, the first criterion to be examined is the condition of the individual companies in terms of absolute volume and volume trends. Within a given industry, certain companies are going to outperform the category in the future. The same sources mentioned earlier (i.e., business periodicals, stock analyst reports, and bank letters) are helpful in analyzing the individual companies.

A second criterion in determining prospect companies is the effectiveness of the marketing and advertising operations of the particular companies. How successful are the company's brands and services versus those of the competition? Does the company have a sophisticated understanding of marketing? What are the backgrounds of the key management people? How much does the company spend on advertising? What is the company's new product record? The answers to these preliminary questions will help determine whether or not a particular company should be an agency prospect.

For each prospect category, the agency should select several companies that represent realistic prospects. This selection should include an appraisal of whether the prospect would consider the agency for its account. For example, if the prospect currently is employing a very large agency and utilizing the many resources available from that agency, it would be unrealistic for a small- to medium-sized agency to consider the company a prospect unless specific information to the contrary existed.

At this point in the six-step process of prospect solicitation, the agency will have constructed a prioritized list of prospect industries, including the names of several prospect companies for each industry. A workable list for a medium- to large-sized agency includes a total of 75 to 100 prospect companies.

Step 4: Review of Each Prospect's History with Agencies

The purpose of step 4 is to eliminate prospects having histories with agencies that indicate they would be undesirable clients. This is a very important step; it can help avoid costly and demoralizing situations.

The first question asked in step 4 is, How many agencies has the client had in the last 10 years? The chances are a client that has had several agencies over a short period of time has inherent problems that disrupt the agency-client relationship and ultimately lead to its severance. Some of these agency hoppers are well-known, while others require some investigative work to uncover. The point is, if a company has a history of unstable agency relationships, chances are the pattern will continue.

The prospect's financial record with agencies should also be examined. What kind of compensation agreement have they sought in the past? What are they willing to spend on production? on collateral materials? The answers to these questions will help determine whether the prospect is really worth pursuing. Certainly, this type of analysis will help prune the prospect list and help avoid potentially costly pursuits.

Finally, the quality of the prospect's advertising product should be investigated. Smart advertising people know that the quality of a company's advertising is at least as much the result of the company's efforts as it is of the agency's efforts. If historically a prospect's advertising has been poor, the chances are that a new agency will be unable to correct the problem.

Exhibit 8–2 summarizes the aspects of a prospect company that should be examined during step 4.

Step 5: Review of the Agency's New Business History

Much can be learned about prospect selection from a review of the agency's record in new business. Therefore, a detailed analysis of the agency's recent history with new accounts should be conducted.

It should be determined how long it typically takes the agency to make a profit on a new account. It is apparent from the number of agencies willing to offer initial bargain rates that many have not established adequate compensation arrangements up front. Many of these bargain arrangements lead to trouble as inevitably the agency learns that it will not profit from the account. The policy of offering reduced rates to lure an account is detrimental to both sides of the agreement. Sooner or later the agency will try to skimp on its services in order to be profitable.

EXHIBIT 8–2
Prospect Factor Analysis

Phase 1

• Company financial position.
• Sales and advertising levels and ratios.
• Growth potential.
• Marketing expertise.
• Product line acceptability.
• International opportunities.
• Current agency situation.
• Personal contacts.
After completion of phase I, worthwhile prospects will emerge from each business category. When they have been established, phase II factor analysis is conducted with this group.

Phase 2

• Current advertising strategy by product/lines.
• Probable target group(s).
• Competitive environment.
  • Spending level/category.
  • Advertising strategies.
  • Long-term opportunities for the industry.
• Other suggested marketing programs.
• New product development.
• Agency situation/evaluation.

An analysis of new accounts should consider how long the average account remains with the agency. In the context of an accurate financial analysis, a good many agencies learn that their new business endeavors have only succeeded in acquiring accounts with very little profit potential.

A historical review of the agency's new business also can indicate the prospects to avoid. If the agency has had trouble with an account because of certain factors inherent to the industry, it can anticipate similar problems with another company in that same industry. If the agency has had trouble handling the diverse needs of an airline account, it would be wise to pass up that category in the future.

The intent of this analysis is in keeping with the purpose of the entire six-step process: to ensure that the prospect list is viable, consisting of worthwhile and realistic prospect companies, while eliminating those that will result in costly and demoralizing efforts on the agency's part.

Step 6: Conflicts in Perspective

Conflicts are here to stay, regardless of wishful thinking on the part of agencies. As long as there are a number of good, solid agencies from which to choose, clients will opt to divide competing products among agencies. It makes sense for clients to encourage competition among similar products; hiring separate agencies is one way to accomplish this. For example, Procter & Gamble has 10 agencies in the United States alone.

Accordingly, conflicts will remain the bane of the new business head's existence. There is a perspective, however, that smart new business operations should have in order to maximize agency growth. Simply stated, an agency should avoid accepting a product from a prospect unless it can become a major agency for that prospect in the future. If more than half of the prospect's products represent conflicts with existing client products, the agency is risking the frustrations and growth limitations that these conflicts will cause since the new client will be limited in the number of assignments it can award.

A long-term perspective will prevent the extremely unpleasant possibility of antagonizing clients by either asking for approval to take on a new business assignment from a competitor or, worse, of informing these existing clients that the agency cannot take on an additional assignment because of a conflict. These situations can seriously undermine the agency-client relationship.

When this six-step process is complete and the prospect list has been developed, it is time to consider how the agency should go about the business of prospect solicitation.

PROSPECT SOLICITATION

An agency cannot rely solely on its reputation to attract prospects. Accordingly, agency management must use every means available to solicit prospective clients, recognizing that most solicitation methods work over the long term, and, like advertising, are an investment intended to reap future rewards for the agency.

Consider, for example, house advertising. It is amazing that in an industry based on the power and effectiveness of advertising, few agencies actually advertise themselves. Part of the reason, no doubt, is the reluctance to spend money on such an effort. Another part of the reason is agency management's inability to agree upon either an advertising strategy or, more often, on the advertising itself. In this case, too many experts are involved with a campaign idea. The way to overcome this part of the problem is for the CEO to work directly with selected creative people on a campaign, recognizing that it is the CEO who eventually must succeed or fail in the new business area. House advertising must flow out of the agency's positioning within the marketplace, as explained in Chapter 1. It should be part of the agency's business plan. It should be strategically sound and should have continuity, two principles that agencies continually remind clients to follow. For example, Young & Rubicam ran a print campaign for many years with the theme line "Resist the Usual." This line was supported by striking visuals. The campaign successfully reinforced the agency's creativity.

An important factor to consider in deciding whether or not to use house advertising is the powerful effect is has on current, as well as prospective, employees. Employees' impressions and understanding of the agency can be aided and abetted by house ads displayed on agency walls.

Another means of prospecting for and soliciting new business is public relations. Most agencies go about this haphazardly, without strategic context or an understanding of the press. The cardinal rule of dealing with the trade press is to be communicative and honest. This does not mean telling the press everything about the agency, but it does mean not lying or misleading the press either. Agencies on which the press can rely in terms of truthfulness and reliability, as well as promptness of response, are those that receive the best press.

The agency's public relations strategy should dovetail with its house advertising strategy, all in the context of the agency's positioning in the marketplace, so that one piece of communication feeds upon the other, regardless of the media in which it appears. It is imperative, therefore, that the CEO is directly involved in both public relations and house advertising. In fact, the public relations officer or the person assigned that responsibility within the agency should report directly to the CEO.

The media are a great source of information for prospect solicitation. All media department members should be urged to seek and relay information related to prospects. Smart agencies also treat the media with respect and professionalism, just as agencies would like their clients to treat them. Inviting the media into the agency for periodic updates can be very fruitful. The media director should be assigned the responsibility of making sure that the media are a great source of new business information.

Speeches can be effective prospecting devices for agencies. Here, too, speeches and the speakers should be working within the context of what the agency is trying to communicate about itself. Haphazard, half-hearted, weak speakers or speeches are counterproductive to the agency's goals. Therefore, a plan for speeches should be devised annually. Target audiences should be selected, and the agency's best speakers should appear before these audiences. The right speech to the right audience can reap enormous benefits for the agency long after the speech has been made.

Concomitant with speeches is agency attendance at important association meetings and conventions. Here, too, attendance should be planned because these meetings can be costly, not to mention the lost time involved. Nevertheless, it is critical that an agency is visible at important meetings and conventions relevant to its current client and prospect lists.

A dramatic means of prospect solicitation is a research study of a top prospect's market. Most clients, whether or not they are happy with their agency lineups, can be induced to listen to an agency's presentation if they believe that some important insights can be obtained. One such study is an industry analysis, which is especially useful if the agency has a variety of prospects within a given industry. A well-conducted survey with follow-up publicity can generate attention within the industry and add to the agency's image of expertise on a particular subject.

It is apparent from the preceding discussion that there are a variety of methods an agency can employ for prospect solicitation. Once again, it is important that these methods are planned within the context of the agency's overall objectives.

NEW BUSINESS PRESENTATIONS

In order to ensure that new business presentations are effective, it is critical that at the outset the agency has a stance, a point of view, a theme that begins, ends, and permeates the presentation. This attitude should derive from the agency's assessment of the key client issue. For example, if a client has an excellent product line but a stodgy image, this should be the focal point of the agency's presentation.

Like all communications, meetings, speeches, and advertising itself, a presentation should be cohesive, dramatic, thorough and, therefore, memorable. In the preceding example, all elements of the presentation should play back to the issue of the client's image.

A cardinal rule of new business presentations is that 95 percent should be devoted to the client's business and 5 percent to the agency's organization. The purpose of the meeting is to enthuse the client about the agency's ability to serve the business. If the client needs to learn more about the agency, ample opportunity exists after the presentation. Therefore, precious time should not be wasted on agency information, which tends to be boring, self-serving, and boastful, when the time can be put to good use in talking about the client's issues and problems.

Regardless of who within the agency analyzes the client's issues and marketing problems, regardless of who comes up with the most insightful strategies for what the client should be doing, regardless of who has the creative insights and prepares the advertising, regardless of who the agency management is and who the department heads are, the agency people who are the best communicators should make the presentation. The prospect's impression of the agency is created in a very short period of time. The client may not necessarily remember who was responsible for agency analysis or preparation, but the presentation will certainly be remembered. Therefore, it behooves the CEO to establish this presentation ground rule up front so that people are not offended when they are not part of the presentation team. The agency CEO should know who within the agency are the most effective speakers and under what circumstances they perform well because the chemistry of the meeting will vary from one prospect to another. The more the agency knows about the prospect's culture and personality, as well as the individuals from the client's organization attending the meeting, the better able the agency will be to cast the meeting correctly.

In a way, nothing an agency does is more unfair than a new business presentation. Because of the emotional nature of a new business presentation, an agency, in just two hours, can convince a client that it is the best agency for that client, when, in reality, it may not be. A prospect might get so caught up in the emotion of the meeting, the ambience of the location, and the skills of the presenters that logic and rational thinking are dismissed. The only way to approach the presentation, then, is to recognize and to take advantage of this fact. One way to take advantage of this situation is to provide a meeting atmosphere within which the prospect will feel most comfortable. The prospect is looking for a new partner and the decision is much the result of the chemistry between the prospect and the agency people in the room. Without a doubt, creative alterations to the room, the use of appropriate props, and a general awareness of the potential effects of the meeting room atmosphere can be rewarding. N. W. Ayer was reported to have converted an entire floor into a J. C. Penney store for the Penney presentation. A few years later, Ayer made a presentation in a Burger King restaurant for that client. The agency won both these very sizeable accounts, although the Burger King business was lost a short time later.

Presentation Participants

Despite the enormous amount of effort that clients expend in the selection of advertising agencies, including the use of consultants, a great deal of prescreening of possible agencies, an elaborate questionnaire, the selection of a limited number of agency finalists, a presentation that may or may not include an elaborate scoring system, and final deliberation among top management about which agency to select, the fact is the presentation itself, because of the emotional nature noted earlier, is often the determining factor in agency selection. This is often unwise and unfair, but it is true. Accordingly, the selection of the agency personnel who will attend the presentation is one of the most critical decisions in the whole area of new business solicitation.

Similar to all aspects of new business solicitation, it is extremely important that the agency has an understanding of what the prospect is seeking in the new agency. For example, the agency should know what services the prospect desires. The degree to which certain services are important to the client will determine the amount of time and effort the agency should spend on these during the presentation itself. If the client is extremely interested in research, then the agency should determine this, then meet this requirement by having an important research executive at the meeting who is prepared to talk about research in the context of the prospect's business needs. Similarly, if the prospect has a particular interest in the utilization of sports programming on TV, then the smart agency will include an expert in this area and will devote an appropriate amount of time to this subject in the presentation in order to demonstrate expertise in this area.

Only proper investigation of the client's needs will determine which of these needs is foremost. This can be the difference between a winning and a losing presentation.

It is paramount, of course, that the CEO attend the presentation meeting. Amazingly enough, this rule is often violated. If the CEO does not attend a new business presentation, it is tantamount to telling the prospect, "We are really not that interested in your business." Most clients realize they will not see much of the CEO once the presentation is over and the business has been assigned, but they do hope to receive the attention and best thinking of the top executives of the agency. It is this very factor that has allowed a great number of smaller agencies to acquire good-sized accounts in recent years.

The CEO performs several duties during the actual meeting. Not only should the CEO of the agency attend the meeting, he or she also should be prepared to talk knowledgably and, of course, enthusiastically about the prospect's business and just what his or her agency can do to help that business. The CEO should open and close the meeting. At the opening of the meeting, he or she outlines agency plans for the presentation, from beginning to end; introduces the key people, mentioning their qualifications for the account; and, in general, sets the tone of the presentation. A weak opening on the part of the CEO often cannot be saved by a brilliant presentation thereafter. At the close of the meeting, the CEO summarizes the key points, including exactly why the agency is the best for the client's particular needs. He or she also should provide the prospect with informational material, such as biographies, summaries of the agency's business analysis, and possibly a list of client references.

The biggest mistake agencies make in terms of who attends a new business meeting is including a variety of department heads, as opposed to the people who actually will be working on the account. Again, most prospects are smart enough to realize they will not see much of the department heads. Therefore, prospects are keenly interested in the key account management, creative, and, possibly, media and research people who will be assigned to their businesses.

Unfortunately, the agency individuals who might be the best long-term performers on the prospect's business are not necessarily the people who will perform best in a one-hour presentation. Therefore, it is paramount that the key individuals involved with a new business presentation are outstanding presenters. Many accounts have not been acquired, despite proper qualifications, because the agency failed to have the right people make the presentation.

Most new business presentations should involve the agency's creative director. It is hard to conceive of a presentation that does not include some display of the agency's creative work. The presence of the creative director further demonstrates the agency's interest in the account. Most likely he or she is also the most articulate exponent of the agency's creative philosophy, something in which all prospects are interested.

In determining who should attend a new business presentation, three rules are recommended. The first is that at least two-thirds of the agency people attending should be those who actually will be assigned to the account. A second rule is that the number attending should not exceed six; any more than six people from the agency can result in a cumbersome and jumbled presentation. A final rule is to never take people to a new business presentation unless they have something important to say. It is embarrassing for both the agency and the client to have people sitting in the meeting who do not participate.

Last Agency or First

Although debatable, the agency that is the last in a series to make a new business presentation may have a distinct advantage. After a number of new business presentations, the distinctiveness of each tends to blur. One agency may even be credited with something that another agency actually said. It is amazing, then, how many agencies fail to ask for the last position. This factor, which may seem tiny in the context of the entire new business process, actually can be the difference between winning and losing a new account.

Examining the Room

Many agency new business presentations are made at the prospect's offices. No agency should make a presentation without first examining the room in which it will be made. The purpose of this examination, which should be done by someone from the agency's TV production department and an account executive or traffic individual, is to make a layout of the room in order to plan for the meeting. Where the agency members will sit, where the prospect will sit, where materials will be shown, where film and/or audio materials will be presented, and generally, the details of the presentation in terms of the limitations of the room are all addressed by this plan. Space, lighting, and sound should also be taken into consideration in preparing for the meeting. Whether or not there is sufficient equipment is important. How much equipment or backup equipment should the agency bring? Should the agency supply a projectionist and/or someone to take care of the lighting?

The agency may have only 30 minutes or so to actually prepare for the presentation in the meeting room. The purpose of investigating and diagramming the room is to ensure that there will be no surprises that might upset the whole meeting. Clients will have no objection to a premeeting investigation. In fact, they will admire the agency's thoroughness.

Product Group Biographies

Whether or not the members of the agency's product group attend the presentation, a booklet including biographies and pictures of the key individuals should be prepared and distributed at the end of the meeting. This is important for several reasons. First, it will be a delineation of the people who will be assigned to the account, including their backgrounds and experience as these relate to the prospect's business. Second, it will act as a reminder of the agency when the prospect's management makes the final decision as to which agency will be appointed. Third, it will be a helpful explanation of the agency's capabilities for those members of the client's organization who did not attend the presentation, but who do have a say in the final decision. Finally, this booklet provides biographies on many more agency people than would be feasible to bring to the meeting itself. Writers, art directors, research, and media individuals, as well as other agency specialists, can be shown in this booklet.

Business Analysis Summary

The successful agency will have done a detailed analysis of the prospect's business. Furthermore, a good deal of the actual presentation must be devoted to discussion of the prospect's business. It is most important that a written summary of the work the agency has done, in terms of analyzing the prospect's business, is left behind for perusal. Because of the time limitations on the presentation itself, it will not be possible for the agency to cover everything it has learned about the client's business. A book, however, can show the thoroughness of the agency's examination of the client's problems. Importantly, it can be passed around to executives who did not attend the presentation. The very permanence of the book has an advantage of reminding people of the agency's presentation. In addition to an analysis of the client's business, the book should include any tentative marketing recommendations.

List of Attendees

A smart practice for the CEO is to hand to each client member a typed list of the people attending from the agency at the beginning of the new business presentation. This list should include names, titles, and a brief summary of each agency individual's background. This list could be accompanied by the agenda for the presentation.

Charts

Any good advertising person knows that good TV communications rely on the linkage of pictures with words. One reinforces the other. In fact, if words and pictures do not reinforce each other, they tend to contradict each other, causing confusion. This is also true of presentations. However, it is surprising how many agencies are lacking in the preparation of visual materials for new business presentations.

Very simply stated, all presenters should have some visual materials to reinforce their words. In terms of charts, the lettering should be a minimum of 2 inches in height. The charts should not repeat word-for-word what the presenter is saying, rather, they should briefly summarize the presenter's key points. A good presenter will quickly review the words on the chart because once the chart is shown, all eyes—and attention—will be on it. In terms of impact, the charts in the presentation are equal to the pictures in a TV commercial. Unfortunately, most agencies do not treat charts with the same degree of attention given TV visuals.

References

The CEO, as part of the closing remarks, should hand a list of client references to the key client individuals. The names of the CEOs of several agency clients should be included. The purpose of this reference list is not only to provide the prospect with some overall references, but also, some references who might comment on the agency's ability to meet the prospect's particular needs or concerns. For example, a prospect with a small budget is always anxious about doing business with a large agency because of concern that the proper amount of attention will not be given the prospect's account. Under such circumstances, the agency should provide the prospect with a list of very satisfied, small clients.

Other times, the prospect might be concerned about the agency's creativity, its research, or a variety of other relevant matters. It is one thing for a prospect to hear how great an agency is from the agency itself, it is another thing to hear it from one of the agency's clients. A good client can help sell the agency.

Satisfied clients should be informed that the agency is using them as references. Most likely, these clients are happy to act on the agency's behalf.

Presentation Follow-Up

The few days between the presentation and the prospect's decision date for agency selection provide the agency with the opportunity for follow-up. The senior agency executive involved (it is hoped the CEO) should meet with the senior prospect executive. The purpose of this meeting is to follow up on presentation information, but, more importantly, to again show enthusiasm for the account. All other factors being equal, the prospect will select the agency that appears to be the most eager to have the prospect's business.

After the Decision

Nothing in the agency business is more exhilarating than a new business win. On such occasions, a celebration is in order—one that includes as many employees as possible. The individuals who played important roles in the win should be singled out and rewarded as an example.

A new business win is an opportunity to develop momentum, which can lead to additional victories. It should be publicized and merchandised as much as possible so that all interested parties, both within and outside the agency, are aware of the agency's victory. A special house ad may be in order. A new business win is a precious circumstance for an agency and should be treated as such.

On the other hand, nothing is more debilitating than a new business loss. A loss can have a strong negative effect on the morale of the agency. As such, it is important that top management deals forthrightly with the issue and communicates to the agency its disappointment, while reassuring agency employees that one event is not controlling and that the agency is alive and well and will have other opportunities in the future. Importantly, subsequent to a new business loss, agency management should look for any positive events affecting the agency. These events present opportunities to create good news about the agency. Most of all, the agency must press on harder than ever in its new business pursuits, recognizing the critical importance of new business to the vitality of the agency.

CHAPTER 9

FINANCIAL MANAGEMENT

ORGANIZATION AND PERSPECTIVE

Several key points have been made in earlier chapters. One of these points is that advertising people are the most important factors in the agency since they create the product. A second point is that the quality of the product helps determine the profits; that is, clients will spend more behind a business-building idea. While agency income and profit levels are affected by client confidence in its advertising, achieving desired agency profitability levels depends mostly on sound agency financial management. This process begins by ensuring that the financial people within the agency are of the highest caliber.

Within any agency or agency office there must be a senior financial executive who is part of the top management team, equal in importance to his or her peers—the heads of the other agency departments and/or functions. The chief financial officer (C.F.O.) must not only be astute in agency financial matters, but must also be informed of the basic workings of an agency. Many financial decisions, particularly in the area of expense management, must be made in the context of the agency's total operation. Therefore, it is critical that the C.F.O. is a member of the agency's operations committee, which is the governing body of day-to-day operations. Accordingly, many of the best agency financial executives are those who "grew up" in the agency business.

The key financial activities to be considered by agency general management are examined in this chapter. This discussion assumes in all cases that the C.F.O. takes the lead in managing these activities. Functions that are purely financial in nature, such as accounting and treasury, and not part of the overall day-to-day management process, are not included here.

This chapter deals primarily with agency profitability and the best way to plan for profitability. Issues that have a bearing on profitability, and that can be controlled by management are also discussed. These issues include individual accountability for profit, client compensation, the profit-and-loss statement, wage freezes as a means of expense control, and employee turnover. Finally, agency profitability trends over the last 10 years are reviewed.

MANAGING PROFITABILITY

Placing or keeping an agency on the path to profitability is the highest priority of agency management. Fortunately, to a very high degree profitability, *can* be managed and an agency should be able to accurately predict its profitability level in any given year, recognizing that one of the critical variables, income, is subject to change, either upward or downward, on short notice. Income changes occur when clients adjust spending plans.

Predicting and managing profitability successfully requires a process. This process must begin at a point in time several months prior to the beginning of the year for which the profit plan is being prepared.

The first step in the process is to establish a realistic income projection for the agency. This requires an account-by-account analysis to arrive at individual account income projections. The senior person responsible for each account should be asked to submit three estimates of account income. The first, a high estimate, assumes that the account will deliver income in line with the best possible circumstances for that account. For example, the forecast might assume that a planned product or line extension will become a reality. This optimistic forecast also might assume that an extra spending test will justify budget increases and the client management will effect these increases.

In another instance, the forecast might assume that business will continue to be good and that this environment will generate advertising reserves.

The second is a low income projection. In contrast to the high estimate, this second projection is based on a pessimistic set of circumstances. Reversals of the examples cited before are anticipated, resulting in advertising budget decreases.

The third forecast and the one used in assembling the agency's total income forecast is the most accurate estimate of the client's income. Falling somewhere between the high and the low estimates, the third projection must be as realistic as possible and, if anything, should be on the conservative or pessimistic side. For example, on a given account, the high estimate might be $8 million, the low might be $2 million, and the most realistic might be $4 million.

Each account should be examined using this first step in the process to arrive at a set of estimates for the agency's entire account list. The grand total of these individual projections represents the best estimate of the agency's total income for the upcoming year.

It is important that top agency management scrutinizes the income forecasts to make sure it is comfortable with the estimated amounts. If there is any doubt, top management should ask the client for an estimate of the account's future size. In this light, top management must know its account managers well enough to recognize who is best at income forecasting and, more importantly, who is continually optimistic in forecasting. This search for accuracy is critically important because the income projection is the number that sets in motion a whole set of agency decisions. If the income forecast turns out to be significantly off (by 10 percent or more), particularly on the downside, the agency can have major financial problems.

At no time during the income-estimating process should assumed income from new business be included. New business income is only real income when the account has been won, the contract has been signed, and the agency knows without doubt that income will materialize.

Once top management is confident that the total income forecast is as realistic as possible, the next step is to determine the desired profitability level for the agency for the upcoming year. This number will be derived primarily from recent agency history, as well as from the profitability goals the agency has set for itself as part of its business planning process. Most agencies set annual profit increase goals of at least 10 percent. An industry standard of profitability success is a 20 percent operating margin; that is, operating expenses should amount at most to 80 percent of operating income. If an agency has been suffering from profitability problems or, in contrast, has seen a strong surge of profitability, then profit goals must be set accordingly.

When profitability goals have been set, the size of the expense budget must be determined. The expense budget is a derivative of the income forecast and the profit goal. While this seems a simple calculation, many agency managements start with the expense base of the prior year and assume increases for the following year. To manage the profitability process effectively, expenses must always be a derivative of the income and profit forecasts. This often forces agency management to make some tough expense decisions, but the truth is expenses must be managed since income is basically a variable that cannot be managed.

To demonstrate the preceding process for managing profitability consider as an example an agency having $50 million in billings. This hypothetical agency has achieved annual profits based on the following:

	Millions of Dollars	
Billings	50.0	
Income	7.5	(assumes income
Expenses	6.0	is 15% of billings)
Operating profit	1.5	

The agency has achieved $1.5 million in operating profit on income of $7.5 million, or a 20 percent level of profit.

Further, assume that for the next year, the best estimate for agency income is $7 million, a decrease of $500,000. Using these figures, two ways of preparing a plan for the next year—the wrong way and the right way—are examined. The wrong way to forecast is to assume that current expenses will be rising at a rate equal to the general inflation rate, say 5 percent. Under these planning assumptions, the agency's profit plan appears as follows:

Millions of Dollars		
Income	7.0	
Expenses	6.3	(assumes a 5% increase)
Operating profit	0.7	

The agency, by letting expenses rise with inflation, has seen its profits decline by more than half from the previous year, from $1.5 million to $700,000. Clearly, this is an unacceptable situation, one with which neither the management nor the stockholders can live.

The right way to prepare the plan is to start with the income forecast of $7 million. The agency made $1.5 million in the base year in this example. For the next year, management sets a goal of a 10 percent increase in profits. This will amount to an additional $150,000 or a total anticipated profit of $1.65 million. Knowing the income forecast and profit goal, the expenses for the next year can now be determined.

Millions of Dollars	
Income	7.00
Expenses	5.35
Operating profit	1.65

In this example, to achieve a profit increase of 10 percent, expenses must be *reduced* from $6 million to $5.35 million. Note the difference between the $5.35 million expense level under one planning system and the $6.3 million expense level when an upward inflationary jump in expenses was assumed.

Obviously, to achieve the higher level of profitability in this example, expenses must be cut from year to year, from $6 million to $5.35 million. To accomplish this, some difficult decisions will have to be made, including the dismissal of some employees. Yet, if the agency is to be successful, it must be profitable, and to be profitable requires some hard choices in controlling expenses.

When faced with an expense budget, management must always make the tough decisions needed to adjust expenses upward or downward according to projected income and profit levels. These decisions, which are essentially payroll decisions, are easier to make when account-by-account profit-and-loss statements are available.

In conjunction with the preparation of the three income forecasts described earlier, each account manager should prepare, with the help of accounting, a profit-and-loss statement for each account for the previous year, plus a projected profit-and-loss statement for the next year using for that purpose the most realistic income forecast and the most recent year's expense base. Since, to a large degree, an agency's total profitability is a function of the combined profitability of its individual accounts, account profitability projections must be a part of the profitability management process.

If it is determined that a particular account is not meeting the agency's profitability objective, which is normally 20 percent of income, management must act to correct the situation. After examining data for the most recent years, agency management must decide how client management will be contacted to attempt to correct the profitability problem. It is important that once it is decided that a meeting with the client is required, the key day-to-day account managers for that client are excluded from the meeting. These managers should be viewed by the client as helpful contributors to the client's business, not as people who are highly concerned with making money. Top agency management or members of the financial function should meet with clients to discuss profitability issues.

Assuming an agency can demonstrate to a client that there is a profitability issue, most clients will be responsive. As good business people they will recognize the need to keep their agencies profitable. If a client does not care if the agency makes money, that client may not be worth keeping.

Agency management should have as a goal a 20 percent profitability level on each and every account. Agencies that rely on certain disproportionately profitable accounts to carry the agency, that is, to make up for the losing accounts, are making a big mistake. If the highly profitable accounts do not deliver these profits in a given year, the agency runs the risk of losing money.

Individual account profitability analyses done in conjunction with a total agency profitability forecast for the next year most likely will require the agency to make some difficult expense decisions. These expense decisions inevitably create difficult personnel decisions since labor costs are by far the biggest cost variable available to agency management. Who to hire, who to fire, who to train, how much to reward are all questions that need to be answered as part of the profit plan for any given year. These decisions must be part of the planning process, not something done in a reactionary fashion as the year progresses.

Update reviews of profitability should be carried out at 90-day intervals as the year progresses. Since each month's passing reduces the time remaining in the year to effect changes in the expense budget, the first 90-day update is the most critical. It is hoped that at that time, more realistic income estimates can be prepared. Having a better fix on the income level for the year will allow agency management to make the expense adjustments needed to maintain the desired profitability level.

Additionally, management must always try to keep expense increases behind any income increases. If the agency is growing and its income is increasing, restricting or delaying expense increases can have dramatic effects on profit levels. For example, assume an agency has a base of $10 million in income, $8 million in expenses, and, therefore, $2 million in operating profit. If, during the year, income rises 10 percent to $11 million and agency management is able to keep expense increases to 5 percent for total expenses of $8.4 million, profits would be $2.6 million, a dramatic increase of 30 percent! A 10 percent income increase, combined with a 5 percent expense increase, results in a 30 percent profit jump.

If, in contrast, income rises 5 percent to $10.5 million and expenses rise 10 percent to $8.8 million, profits actually *decline*

15 percent to $1.7 million. Thus, seemingly small percentage differences in income and expense levels can have major effects on profit levels.

One way agencies have restricted profitability levels in recent years is by allowing another expense variable —rent—to get out of control. In the last 10 years, as a percentage of income rent has more than doubled, from a range of 3–5 percent to a range of 6–10 percent or more. While timing is a big and uncontrollable variable in making rental decisions, many agencies have erred simply by paying too much rent and by signing long-term leases that have the effect of mortgaging the future of the agency. Clients do not switch agencies because of an address or living quarters. More likely, clients think less of an agency with extravagant office surroundings. Clients are going to ask who is paying for the environment, with the inevitable answer that they, the clients are. As with all business elements, real estate has cycles of ups and downs, and agencies must be careful to avoid long-term commitments at the top of these cycles. Most likely, these can only be avoided with the help of outside expert legal and real estate counsel since it is unlikely that agency management will have the expertise to make these very important rental decisions independently.

Besides labor and rent, most other agency expense categories are derivatives of basic labor costs. People use the supplies, take the trips, and entertain the clients.

Basically, any reduction in labor costs will indirectly lower the overhead component of agency costs. The typical ratio is that one dollar of direct labor expense generates another dollar of overhead cost. Again, the high priority is for agency management to manage labor expenses. As demonstrated, the profitability rewards from successfully doing so are enormous.

INDIVIDUAL ACCOUNTABILITY

There was a time when agencies could not determine individual account profitability. Total income and expenses were known for the agency and the resulting total agency profitability derived from these figures. While income amounts for individual accounts were available, the means for allocating expenses account by account were unavailable. As a result, individuals could not be held accountable for account profitability, nor were they concerned with account profitability since they derived no benefit from it. Their only goal was to make clients happy, and they would exert only whatever effort was necessary to achieve that end. Only a few at the very top of the agency cared about expenses, and they only cared about total expenses, not individual account expenses.

As computers became more useful and as both clients and agencies became more interested in knowing the details of account profitability, processes were developed to that end. Today, all agencies have the ability to determine how much each account makes or loses. In addition, since many clients tailor their compensation policies according to agreed-upon levels of profitability, often client and agency together review the details of account profit-and-loss statements.

Accordingly, the next tier of agency management has become involved in all aspects of individual account profitability. Certainly, department heads want to know how their personnel is being allocated, account by account. People with overall individual account responsibility now assume profitability to be part of that responsibility. Top management, more than anyone, is interested in individual account profitability in order to know which accounts are providing the profits and which accounts need to be addressed in order to correct an unprofitable situation.

Agencies have failed to place profit accountability with the people responsible for the day-to-day account activities. These individuals could be rewarded according to the levels of profitability achieved. Management supervisors, for example, should have bonus rewards based on levels of profitability. The point here is to reward the people who have the most control over personnel and other expenditures associated with the day-to-day handling of an account. If these management supervisors know that their own compensation is affected by account profitability, they will be vitally concerned with expense control and will be less willing to send extra people on trips, to put unnecessary people in meetings, or to expend extra out-of-pocket monies on clients.

The argument against placing accountability with the people responsible for day-to-day account activities is that by overly reducing expenses, the quality of the agency's performance suffers over time. The net effect is a short-term increase in profitability followed by a decrease in agency quality and the possibility of undermining the client relationship. There are, however, two ways to avoid this risk. First, top management has the means to oversee accounts both from a quality and a profitability standpoint. They have the means of balancing the need for profitability vis-à-vis the need for agency quality. Second, management supervisors must be made to understand that it is possible to deliver high quality and at the same time manage expenses to improve profitability.

Granted, there are variables beyond the control of anyone at the agency—variables that can greatly affect account profitability. Sudden increases or decreases in billings, the need for a new campaign, or the introduction of a line extension are just a few of the uncontrollable events that can alter account profitability. These events, however, will occur regardless of how far down in the agency profit accountability is placed. The potential benefits of rewarding middle management based on account profitability outweigh the risks of acting in this fashion. Without doubt, profitability-based bonuses represent a potential for significantly increasing individual account profitability and therefore overall agency profitability.

CLIENT COMPENSATION

It is old news that the 15 percent commission system is outdated, even though a large number of clients cling to this system either wholly or with some variation. Agencies by and large favor the 15 percent method because it has served them well from a profitability standpoint. It is simple and it keeps clients out of decision making with regard to the expenditure of agency resources.

Yet, inevitably it seems that new compensation practices will prevail, and the 15 percent system will all but disappear. The question is, what is the best alternative method?

Many clients for some time have experimented with and/or adopted a spectrum of compensation systems. These systems have been described in detail, along with their plusses and minuses, and are available both from the 4As and the ANA. It is fair to say that the ultimate compensation system will have three primary components.

First, the agency will be compensated for direct costs and overhead on the business. The agency, therefore, will know it cannot lose money on the business.

Second, the agency's profit will be determined by an agreed set of performance criteria. These criteria will be a combination of judgmental and measurable factors. Possible criteria include the following:

Judgmental
Quality of agency product (function by function)
Quality and continuity of agency personnel
Top management involvement
Measurable
Sales
Share of market
Copy research factors
Consumer awareness and attitudes

Third, all components of the agency (advertising, sales promotion, direct marketing, public relations, etc.) will be compensated on the same basis. This will eliminate any incentive the agency might have to recommend a particular form of communication.

From these three factors, it is apparent that a fee-based system will prevail, one that compensates an agency by fees related to the personnel resources the agency expends on an account. This system includes a profitability provision as well. Despite its disadvantages—mainly in the areas of excess record keeping, negotiation, and analysis—and the reduction in incentives for the agency to initiate special efforts, the fee system does compensate the agency for its employee utilization and is more like the systems found in other professional, people-intensive fields, such as law and architecture.

Most importantly, the "ideal" system outlined will only succeed if the incentive component is effective—that is, it provides the agency with realistic and significant rewards for outstanding performance; creates a set of shared goals for client and agency alike; and the compensation system eliminates any agency prejudice toward a particular communication skill or discipline so that the client is confident the agency is being objective in its recommendations.

PROFIT-AND-LOSS STATEMENT

Exhibit 9–1 shows a prototypical profit-and-loss statement for an agency. It assumes that agency revenues are 15 percent of billings. All other percentages are based on revenues of 100

EXHIBIT 9–1
Prototypical Profit-And-Loss-Breakdown

	Percent[1]
Billings	100
Revenues	15
Salaries	40
Other operating expenses	37
Operating profit	23
Service fees	3
Operating profit before bonuses	20
Bonuses	5
Operating profit after bonuses	15
Nonoperating expenses	3
Profit before taxes	12
Taxes	6
Profit after taxes	6

[1]Except for billings and revenues, all percentages are based on revenues. Revenues are assumed to be 15 percent of billings.

percent. The numbers clearly show the dominance of labor as a percentage of expenses. In this example, labor expenses amount to 40 percent of total expenses.

Most other operating expenses are either directly or indirectly driven by labor. They include travel, telephone, entertainment, supplies, rent, and all other expenses related to the day-to-day operation of an agency. Service fees assume the agency is part of an agency network and therefore must pay fees to the corporation for services the agency has received, such as for accounting or account coordination.

The 5 percent bonus shown in Exhibit 9–1 is consistent with the current level of overall bonus for an entire agency. This bonus is also extended to clerical and secretarial staff.

Nonoperating expenses are those not related to day-to-day operations. These primarily include interest expense.

A profit of 12 percent before and 6 percent after taxes is consistent with the norm. If computed on the basis of billings, profit after taxes is in the range of 1 percent.

EXPENSES CONTROLLED BY WAGE FREEZES

One way agencies can control expenses is to institute a wage freeze, the act of maintaining all salaries at a constant level for a period of time in order to hold down expenses. This is a mistake. First, across-the-board wage freezes reduce management flexibility to reward people when they should be rewarded. Second, wage freezes create a mentality that says everyone will be treated alike. Third, when a wage freeze is relaxed, a great deal of pent-up demand is released, which, if met, can quickly undo all the benefits of the freeze in the first place.

Middle management, including functional heads, should agree with top management on total expense budgets. These managers should then be given the flexibility to allocate their budgets according to the needs of the business as these people see them. If they wish to give a deserving employee a 20 percent raise and the total budgeted expense increase is just 5 percent, they will have to find ways to accommodate the 20 percent increase. This can be done by giving raises of less than 5 percent or no raises at all to some employees or by eliminating jobs either by firing or through normal attrition. Even in dire times, the managers closest to the day-to-day realities of assessing employee performance must be given the flexibility to reward as they see fit, while staying within the total operating budget. Nothing is more demoralizing, in good or bad times, than an employee attitude that all employees are being treated the same. It destroys the incentive to perform and has the most detrimental effect on the very best people.

EMPLOYEE TURNOVER

Turnover is the annual percent change in employee personnel. Turnover can be measured by function, by level, by department or by total agency. It is an important criterion for measuring change within the agency and can be a strong positive or negative indicator of agency morale.

A healthy overall turnover percentage for an agency is in the area of 10 to 15 percent. Importantly, however, it is not the number per se, but the quality of the turnover that is critical. One signal is given when an agency has a small turnover percentage, but the entire turnover results from the departure of the best and most senior creative people. Another signal is given when the turnover is reasonable, say 10 percent, but consists totally of younger people with two to three years with the agency. No turnover at all is usually a negative indication. While it suggests loyalty, it also indicates stagnation.

Once a year top management should review three-year trends in turnover as part of its overall review of the state of the agency during the business planning process. Carefully examined, function by function, level by level, and over a period of years, turnover levels can provide excellent insight into the quality of agency personnel and, more importantly, aid in the planning and decision making of the most critical subject of all, personnel management.

AGENCY PROFIT LEVELS AND TRENDS

While much publicity has been given to the tendency of clients to seek their alternative (lower) compensation arrangements with their agencies, agency profitability levels have not suffered in any significant way. Exhibit 9–2 shows ten-year (1978–1987) profit levels as reported by the 4As. While the year 1978 shows the highest level, 17.9 percent, the profit level has remained basically between 10 percent and 15 percent. The ups and downs in operating profit percentages are more likely a result of changing business conditions, not changes in client compensation arrangements.

Exhibit 9–3 provides additional data for the same ten-year period, particularly expense data. It can be seen that with few exceptions the major categories of expenses have remained more

EXHIBIT 9–2
Operating Profit Trends (1978–1987)

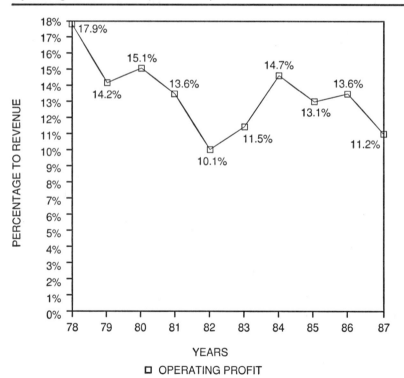

EXHIBIT 9–3

1978–1987 Profit and Cost Trends (All Data Percentage To Revenue)

	1978	1979	1980	1981	1982	1983	1984	1985	1986	1987
Operating profit	17.9%	14.2%	15.1%	13.6%	10.1%	11.5%	14.7%	13.1%	13.6%	11.2%
Expense trend	59.1%	62.2%	60.6%	60.5%	62.7%	61.2%	59.0%	58.9%	56.5%	59.8%
Total payroll										
Space and facilities	12.1%	12.4%	11.9%	13.1%	14.1%	13.8%	12.9%	14.7%	15.1%	15.4%
Client service expense	4.9%	4.2%	4.9%	5.7%	5.9%	6.3%	6.0%	6.3%	6.7%	5.2%
Corporate expenses	4.9%	5.1%	5.5%	5.5%	4.9%	5.0%	5.1%	4.1%	6.0%	5.5%
Professional fees	1.2%	2.0%	1.9%	1.7%	2.3%	2.2%	2.2%	2.9%	2.3%	2.8%
Total expenses	82.1%	85.8%	84.9%	86.4%	89.9%	88.5%	85.3%	86.9%	86.4%	88.8%

Note: For the years 1978–1981, the data used is from the category of agencies with gross income of $13,500M – $30,000M. In 1982, for the first time, the information was available for agencies with gross income of $30,000M – $75,000M so in the years 1982 – 1987, the data used is from this category.

Source: All data from AAAAs.

or less steady. For example, the biggest expense category of all, total payroll, has remained very close to 60 percent. Space and facilities have grown almost 3 percent during the ten-year period, directly attributable to rent increases. There is also an increase in professional fees over the period, reflecting additional consulting, accounting, and legal activities. However, the overall total for this category is small.

The data indicate that agencies have managed to keep costs in line despite reduced client income resulting from alternative compensation systems. What the data do not show are some hidden expense reductions that the agencies have effected in order to maintain margins. Most significant of these is the reduction in training efforts. No meaningful data exist on agency training costs. Nevertheless, agencies generally have not devoted the time and money to this activity that they once did. Over the long term, this will have a detrimental effect on the quality of agency services. Agencies that continue training efforts will have an advantage over their competitors. Not only will they have a more professional staff, but also a more loyal staff since employees think very highly of employers who provide training. As noted in Chapter 4, agencies should provide annual training experiences for all professional employees.

A final thought on agency profitability. If clients persist in driving down agency compensation and agencies persist in maintaining profit margins by driving down expenses, then agency service quality will suffer. This situation is a little like the maple syrup manufacturer who each year takes a little maple sugar out of the product. Compared with the previous year, the quality difference is undetectable, but over time, the product difference from the first year to the tenth year can be disastrous. Agencies have maintained margins for 10 years even though clients have reduced compensation. Sooner or later agency quality must suffer, which is not in the best interest of clients in the long run.

CHAPTER 10

MANAGEMENT ISSUES

This book is devoted to the major areas of concern to agency management. Each chapter covers a primary management subject, but there are a variety of other smaller, yet important, issues with which agency management must contend. There are also subjects of interest to management and to those hoping to achieve agency management positions. This chapter deals with these subjects and issues, including the influence of management attitudes and behavior; desired qualities of agency management; criteria of a successful management meeting; the role of internal and external communication and, particularly, communication concerning the creative output of the agency; an approach to creative awards; and, finally, politics within an advertising agency.

MANAGEMENT ATTITUDE AND BEHAVIOR

By its attitudes and behavior, the management of an advertising agency sets the tone for the entire agency. There are many substantive issues that agency management must confront and direct in running the agency, management subjects such as determining the correct positioning for the agency; developing an effective business plan; correctly structuring the organization; managing the three key areas of people, product, and profit; and astutely attending to agency growth. All these substantive issues are addressed earlier in this book. Yet, often the less substantive, more stylistic areas, such as management's attitude and behavior, have dramatic effects on the fortunes of the agency. This is because no matter how many plans, policies, processes, and procedures an agency has, unless the agency management provides leadership by its daily actions, expressions, and mannerisms, the agency will not prosper. For example, if the agency is supposed to care about its people, but the agency management rarely leaves its offices to mix with the people in the other parts of the agency, it is unlikely agency personnel will think of management as caring.

Management must understand that employees observe carefully, looking for signals and directions to follow. People want to be led, and they want to be part of a successful organization. Management that preaches and practices professionalism of the highest order will find that its employees will respond accordingly, but if management preaches one way and practices another, employees will become disillusioned and demoralized and the agency's efforts will suffer accordingly. For example, if agency management professes to believe that the key to the success of the agency is the quality of the agency's creative product and that profits will flow from creative success, but then behaves and acts on a day-to-day basis as though the only thing that counts is profitability, then employees will become rightfully cynical as to the true intentions of the management.

So it is with all elements of agency management. All professed policies and plans must be backed by agency management behavior consistent with these policies and plans. One good way to monitor behavior is for management to self-assess its actions, individually and collectively, as part of the annual business planning process. The business planning meetings, after all, are intended to be candid examinations of all aspects of the agency. What better time to evaluate the management.

In the final analysis, it is the responsibility of the top agency officer and his or her closest subordinates to set the tone for the entire agency through their leadership.

QUALITIES OF AGENCY MANAGEMENT

What does it take in terms of personal qualities to succeed in the management of an advertising agency? What are the unique characteristics needed to manage an agency?

It is assumed that if an individual is even being considered for a management position, he or she will have proven him- or herself more than adequately in a number of dimensions, particularly in intelligence, interpersonal abilities, and communication skills. Intelligence, as a requisite, speaks for itself in any business endeavor. However, the mind that can best prosper in an advertising environment is unique; it is curious, analytical, and creative.

Managers must be curious because the business of advertising relies on and is essentially about human behavior in the broadest sense. Caring about and knowing as much as possible about why different people behave as they do, therefore, is critical to success. Every product or service that an agency represents is an opportunity to delve into the many aspects of human behavior related to that product or service. This opportunity to observe human reactions to a wide variety of products and services is one of the advantages of a career in advertising.

Second, a manager must have an analytical mind because the nature of advertising requires the ability to constantly draw conclusions from a myriad of evidence, some of which is substantive and reliable, some of which is more qualitative and assumptive. This process is brought to bear across a wide spectrum of situations, from determining copy strategy on a brand to reading a financial statement.

Lastly, a creative mind is an essential management characteristic because creativity is what the advertising business is all about. A creative mind is defined as one that, after absorbing and digesting a great deal of information, can then translate that material into unique and surprising solutions. This mental process must basically apply to the act of creating and evaluating advertising, but also has broad application to the day-to-day activities of the agency, such as determining the proper staffing on an account or providing marketing guidance to a client. A creative mind will help here, too.

Interpersonal abilities, the second human dimension without which a person would not get to a management position, takes many forms. This is because to succeed in an agency, an individual must obtain the confidence and respect of three constituencies: peers, management, and clients. Accordingly, an individual must be able to relate effectively to a spectrum of personalities. Peers include not just those in the person's particular function—say account management—but also in the other functions (creative, media, research, and administrative) with whom the person must deal in the course of everyday business.

As different as people are in personality and behavior *within* the agency, so, too, are the clients, whose respect must also be gained. In addition, to be promoted an individual must have the blessings and support of management, and therefore must be able to relate to these usually older, more experienced people. The upshot is that the individual must genuinely enjoy talking to and working with an enormous range of people so respect, if not friendship, is earned from all.

Excellent communication skills, coupled with the particular kind of intelligence described before, and strong interpersonal abilities are also basic characteristics necessary for early success in the agency business. Written communication skills include letter and document writing, not copy writing, and written communication, both within the agency and to the client. The ability to write clear, concise letters, reports, and documents is essential to early success in advertising, particularly in account management. However, simply because of the time devoted to oral communication (5 to 10 times more than to written communication) an individual must develop the ability to speak clearly and effectively in order to succeed. This skill must be developed to a high level in one-on-one situations, in small groups, and in large groups. An individual should always strive to improve his or her speaking abilities, whatever the job level.

What, then, are the qualities over and above these basics that are required to succeed in agency top management? There are likely five: vision, integrity, a willingness to give credit to others, a sense of humor, and stamina.

The need for a *vision*—a set of goals, a perspective about what the agency is all about—is essential to the success of any organization. The clearer the vision, the more inspiring, the more consistent and repetitive in its telling, the more the agency will respond and the higher the level of excellence the agency will achieve. Chapter 1 describes vision in the context of positioning the agency competitively. This vision must come from and be articulated by management.

Integrity exists in two forms: professional and personal. Professional integrity at any stage of an individual's career is that person's commitment to excellence. At the management level, professional integrity encompasses the agency's entire product and evolves from a commitment to what is right for the clients, not just expedient or right for the agency. Professional integrity is concerned with the agency's total level of professionalism, because if management is willing to cut corners, live with weak strategies, or sell mediocre advertising to its clients, agency people will sense this attitude and reflect it in their own work, bringing down the whole agency's level of performance.

Personal integrity, as contrasted with professional integrity, is the quality of relating directly, honestly, and consistently over time to fellow employees, as well as to clients. Personal integrity is the single most important quality necessary to building trust between people. It is also critical to the reduction of politics within the agency; politics are the enemy of good agency management.

Integrity boils down to the need for people to believe in their management (as leaders), to be able to take at face value their management's words on subjects that really count, such as the state of the agency, the course of the agency, the commitment of the agency, and, number one of all, their own careers. A waffling, inconsistent, if not outright deceptive agency manager or management will eventually be done in by the agency people. The trust that comes from management's integrity cannot be measured, but is unquestionably an essential ingredient to greatness—of the individual manager and of the agency itself.

There are a lot of egos in agencies, and, generally speaking, this is a good thing as long as ego gratification does not get out of hand. The need to recognize egos and performances is ongoing. The best managers will do this on a fair and consistent basis, often without taking credit themselves. The weak manager will take disproportionate credit for good events, while laying the blame for bad events on his or her people. A weak collection of managers will compete amongst themselves for credit and hide when blame is due. Therefore, a manager who is willing to let others *share the credit,* while taking the blame him- or herself, will stand out as a strong leader and will be respected for his or her fairness.

A fourth required quality for successful advertising management is a *sense of humor.* Advertising is a form of art; it is basically immeasurable and largely judged according to the eye of the beholder. Considering the number and variety of people both within and without the agency involved in the process of creating, evolving, and approving advertising, and adding to that the huge stakes involved in terms of money and careers, it is not surprising that stress is a constant. The individual who takes all this stress to heart, if not to stomach, is not going to make it in the advertising business. Since the amount of stress increases proportionately with responsibility, it follows that the best managers will have the sense of humor to deal with stress. Being a student of human nature, recognizing the foibles of people, and being able to put these into an amusing context without becoming too cynical, is essential to the success and enjoyment of being a manager. To the attentive observer, there are numerable humorous situations in an advertising environment, and these are big plusses in an advertising career.

Stamina is included as a required managerial quality because an agency management position just plain requires it. Considering the hours, the essentially stressful nature of the business, and, in most cases, the amount of travel involved, both mental and physical fatigue are constant dangers. Therefore, current and future agency managers should recognize this problem and take steps to deal with it. Not surprisingly, these steps include good planning and scheduling, having other outside interests and making the time to enjoy those interests, and finally, keeping in shape, both mentally and physically.

AGENCY MANAGEMENT MEETINGS

It is essential for agency managers to hold periodic off-campus meetings to resolve problems, to discuss and formulate plans, to communicate information, and, generally, to rally agency individuals for the future. A management meeting, in this case, is defined as any meeting that includes the agency's top management and a representation of other people from within the agency. Typically, the meeting includes the top echelon of the agency, plus the next 10 to 20 percent of the people who run the agency day to day.

Any management meeting, whether it involves an individual office or a group of offices, can be evaluated using criteria that are measurable (at least in subjective terms). It is even possible to measure these criteria on a scale of 1 to 5 and to actually arrive at a rough score, if you will, as to how successful the meeting has been. If this is done on a consistent basis over time, it is possible to improve meetings considerably and on a measurable basis. Following are these management meeting criteria. The criteria must be evaluated from the standpoint of the attendees, exclusive of top management.

The first criterion for evaluating an agency meeting is whether it is evident that members of management care and are involved in the agency. This is demonstrated at a meeting quite simply by the participation of the management in the meeting itself, as well as in the nonmeeting events, including evening activities. If members of management just show their faces, make a few remarks, and then are not seen again, they signal to those present that management is not involved and does not much care about what is happening to the agency.

A second criterion is whether management has a plan for the agency, a set of goals to be achieved and to be made known to the entire agency.

Third criterion is a clearly conveyed feeling that management cares about the individuals present.

Another criterion is that at the end of the meeting, people depart feeling they are better informed as a result of the meeting.

The fifth criterion is that there are clear, actionable steps to be taken as a result of the meeting.

Another management criterion is that the meeting is successful in terms of location, meeting content, and overall ambience, including any sports and/or social activities.

The last criterion is client involvement. The question of client attendance depends upon subject matter. If the presence of

EXHIBIT 10–1
Criteria for Evaluating an Advertising Agency Management Meeting

1. Management cares and is involved in the agency, as demonstrated by its participation in the meeting itself, including the evening events.
2. Management has a plan—it has specific goals. Management has a clear perspective on where the agency is going, how the agency should be positioned, and how the agency is going to get there. The agency is a good place to be because management is in control.
3. Management knows who I am as an individual, it cares about me.
4. Attendees are better informed about what is happening in the agency as a result of the meeting. There is little or no flimflam.
5. Attendees have actionable steps as a result of the meeting. There is a timetable, tasks to be done, and clear responsibilities.
6. The location, the selection, and the scheduling of events (meeting, athletic, social) were all well done.
7. Clients were involved in the meeting.

a client restricts open participation by the attendees or if the subject matter is highly confidential, then, perhaps, the client should be excluded. However, the agency business is a service business, and the attendance of a client or two represents reality. Perhaps a client can be brought in to reinforce some point management wants to emphasize. An invitation to a meeting might be extended to make a client feel closer to the agency by being involved in an important agency event.

Exhibit 10–1 is a seven-point recap of the preceding criteria. As suggested, a point measurement scale of 1 to 5 can be used to evaluate the meeting for each criteria and for the total meeting itself.

COMMUNICATION

Being in the communication business, it is expected that advertising agencies would be particularly adept at managing their own communication. Most agencies, however, are not.

Two basic categories of communication are important to agencies: external and internal. While there is overlap between the two in terms of subject matter, it is important to recognize that the external and internal audiences are divergent in terms of information needs. Therefore, these audiences require separate communication strategies, plans, and executions. Also because of these differences, the individual responsible for external communication requires different skills and experience from those of the person managing the internal communication program. Each of these communication needs is examined.

The key external audiences are the press, business prospects, clients, and prospective employees. In addition, people in the media are an important audience since the attitudes these media people have and the information they convey often influence events.

The individual responsible for external communication must bring the agency's marketing perspective to the job. Unless the communication director completely understands for what the agency stands and how it wants to be positioned within the market structure, he or she cannot do an effective job. It is hoped, therefore, that the external communication director will have had some hands-on marketing experience and/or training. In small agencies and branch offices of big agencies the communication task will have to be assumed as an added responsibility by one of the key executives of the agency. Most likely, only a large agency can afford a full-time communication director.

External communication requires expert knowledge and experience with the press, often a small group of individuals who control the major sources of information on the subject of advertising. The press includes the key people in the advertising trade press, as well as individuals responsible for marketing and advertising columns in the important mass media. An excellent agency communication director, over time, will develop a rapport with these key media people. It is hoped the people from the press will develop respect for the agency's communication director as the result of being treated in an open, forthright, and honest fashion. Since members of the press, particularly within the advertising trade sector, are often changing, it is a never-ending job to maintain these personal relationships.

Knowing the people of the press and understanding the marketing objectives of the agency allows the communication director to effectively accomplish the external communication task. For example, if the agency is trying to position itself as the number one agency in the market in terms of its capacity to generate ideas, then all information should be provided in the context of projecting a particular creative image of the agency to its key audiences—prospective clients and employees. Of course, current clients and employees will be exposed to this communication as well. The important goal is to ensure that each story or article feeds a specific creative point of view about the agency so that prospective clients and employees will have a more positive and receptive attitude about the agency's creativity.

Internal communication is an easier agency task because there is only one audience: current employees. Here, too, communication must be within the context of an overall agreed-upon goal, which is again related to the positioning of the agency. Beyond this, the objective of internal communication is to continually convey to the existing agency staff all pertinent information related to the agency's product, clients, and, most important of all, employees. Agency employees have a great interest in their fellow workers. Information about individual business successes, as well as personal information unrelated to the job, is useful. This information creates a feeling of family by allowing the people to get to know one another in timely and interesting ways.

The person charged with the internal communication task should be creative. He or she should be able to continually develop new, different, and fun ways to talk to the employees. These ways of communicating internally go beyond the printed word to include special internal meetings, events, and parties, like the annual Christmas party or a summer picnic. A truly effective internal communication director barrages the employees with a variety of positive messages through memos, newsletters, and bulletins, weekly if not daily.

Separate from external and internal communication needs, the media are an important agency audience because they have the means and opportunity to influence an agency's reputation. They also often have vital information about clients and people. Therefore, it behooves agencies to communicate with the media. In addition to the many one-on-one or small-group opportunities that exist for this purpose, agencies should consider periodic media-orientation meetings aimed at both informing and entertaining the media. Since media people spend so much of their time soliciting agency business, reversing the process can have a dramatic effect and can even turn media people into agency ambassadors.

In summary, a strong communication program can greatly enhance the agency's reputation in the marketplace and can bolster employee attitudes about the company for which they work. Therefore, communication must be an important part of the annual planning process for agency management.

COMMUNICATION AND MERCHANDISING OF CREATIVE WORK

Within any given agency, if the professional staff was asked to name the agency's clients and to describe the agency's creative work on behalf of these clients, feedback would be startlingly poor. Similarly, if the agency's clients were asked the same questions, the answers would be even more dismal. Agency personnel and clients are usually ignorant of the agency's client list and creative product for the simple reason that agencies do not effectively communicate and merchandise this information.

Yet, the means to effectively communicate this information are readily available. Some of these means are employed from time to time by agencies. Few agencies, however, systematically or relentlessly pursue this worthwhile objective.

The following are some of the proven techniques for making employees and clients more aware of the agency's clients and creative product. The end result of this communication is to make employee and client alike more informed, comfortable, and even proud of the agency.

These techniques are recommended for communicating to employees:

- As part of new employee indoctrination, present a client list and a wide selection of the agency's work.

- Display advertising around the agency. Update these displays frequently. Particularly, utilize waiting areas by elevators. Station a continuous-loop videotape there.
- As part of all employee meetings, include an update of the agency's creative work.
- At least twice a year have an agencywide meeting, with major emphasis on the agency's creative output and clients.
- Create an employee weekly newsletter that emphasizes the agency's advertising.
- Create a permanent employee brochure (which can be updated) that features the agency's clients and work.
- Create monthly awards for the best advertising for each medium. Prominently display these advertisements and awards around the agency.
- Invite client guest speakers to as many agency functions as possible.

When communicating to clients, the following are recommended:

- Instill the need for all professional-level employees to merchandise the agency's client list and product to all clients. Have a kickoff meeting.
- Include the agency's other work as appropriate in client meetings.
- Share agency brochures, periodicals, and newsletters with clients.
- Several times per year, hold meetings and social functions involving all clients. Show the agency's creative work at these gatherings.

The end result of all these efforts is that both employees and clients are enthusiastic ambassadors of the agency.

CREATIVE AWARDS

Related to communicating the agency's creative product to its audience is the subject of creative awards. Agencies have different attitudes concerning the many awards given for creative work. Clients have yet another perspective. While clients are generally pleased if their creative works receive recognition, they are much more interested in whether or not their advertising is working in the marketplace. Moreover, if a client's business situation is not sound, winning an award could have a negative effect on the agency relationship. Clients suspect that many creative people are more driven by a desire to win a creative award than to create business-building ideas. These suspicions often are justified. Creative people know that their careers can be greatly enhanced by an award. What, then, should agency management's attitude be with regard to creative awards?

Despite the cynicism many felt for creative awards, an agency, for several reasons, should participate in contests aggressively, yet thoughtfully. The first and obvious reason is to placate the creative people who want to win awards. An agency that shuns awards altogether will not be able to attract and keep the best creative people. Therefore, agencies should invest the time and money to participate in award contests.

Another, more important, reason an agency should aggressively pursue awards is the positive effect winning can have on the agency's reputation. Just a few wins can greatly enhance the agency's fame and make it more attractive to its key audiences—its employees and clients. Several big creative awards can catapult an agency to the top of the industry. Therefore, it behooves agencies to select the current clients having the greatest potential for exceptional advertising and to then devote the appropriate creative resources to those clients. For once a solid creative reputation has been secured by an agency, the effects can be long lasting, even for a decade or more. The rewards from awards justify management's attention to them.

POLITICS

Divisive politics are the enemy of effective advertising management. They can undermine an agency operation and even cause business losses.

It is natural in a people-intensive business, such as advertising, that relationships exist. In fact, it is relationships on the job that create the agency's end product. One of the major advantages of being in the advertising business is the frequency with which business relationships grow into personal ones. Although this phenomenon can be found in other industries, it is intensified in the advertising business, where the end product is intangible and much the result of employee collaboration.

When, however, relationships reach the point where they have as their objective personal gain independent of the agency's overall objectives, they are destructive. These negative political relationships exist in several forms.

One simple form is politics that develop when an individual uses contacts within the agency for personal gain. An example is a newer employee who, because of a contact he or she has made with a member of management, receives undue credit, whether monetarily, in the form of promotion, or in some more subtle fashion, such as being selected for an important agency task force. When this happens, the favored individual's peers take note and conclude that there are other ways to get ahead in the agency besides talent and hard work. Too many instances of a similar nature will result in a general consensus that getting ahead requires having a friend in management. Obviously, there sometimes is a subtle difference between getting ahead or being promoted because the individual has a contact in top management and getting ahead because management recognizes the individual deserves to move up. However, the agency mainstream is quite adept at detecting these subtleties.

A second form of negative politics, one that is more harmful to an agency's operation, involves the collaboration of a group of people on something that will benefit the group, but not necessarily the agency. An example is a group who decide that having an individual, most likely one of them, in a particular job (say, associate creative director) will help all of them. So, having decided this, they politic individually and as a group, to achieve this goal. Here, too, there is a subtle difference between a group of people championing the cause of someone truly deserving of promotion and a movement to place someone in a job despite the fact that the person is not ready for the responsibility. Here, also, the agency mainstream will detect the difference and react accordingly.

Another form of negative politics occurs when a relationship with a client is used to further personal aims, despite the effects of such action upon the overall agency. For example, a copywriter befriends the client marketing director and uses the relationship to get ahead. Whether done in concert with an unknowing or a knowing client, the results are similar. If this type of politics becomes widespread, the cumulative effect can be demoralizing. Over a period of time, these politics breed an attitude that creating and selling great advertising is secondary to developing client "friends."

All forms of negative politics can be controlled, if not eliminated, by strong top management and particularly by an alert C.E.O. who reacts quickly and decisively against these activities. Proper management actions will give clear signals to the agency that politics are not allowed. In the case of individual attempts at using contacts within the agency to get ahead, the C.E.O. and the management team must ensure that agency systems and procedures result in the rewarding and promotion of only those people most deserving.

When people band together for their own self-serving purpose, management must put a stop to it through forceful action, often by firing one or more of the group. When agency individuals use client contacts to disproportionately aid their own careers, agency management must, through their own knowledge of and contacts with the client, nip these conspiracies early by confronting the guilty parties and by expressing, in no uncertain terms, the agency's attitude about politics.

Avoidance of politics is a primary management goal. If agency management is alert to the danger signs of politics and is quick to react against them, the negative impact of these politics can be largely avoided.

Nepotism, the hiring of relatives, while not necessarily political in nature, can have an equally damaging effect upon the agency. When relatives, whether competent or not, are put in professional-level jobs at an agency, mainstream agency people conclude that getting ahead is not necessarily a function of talent. Widespread nepotism will have a serious negative effect on the agency. In fact, the best agencies enforce policies barring nepotism in all forms.

CHAPTER 11

THE FUTURE

In looking back over the history of the advertising business, it is possible to observe a number of trends; trends so strong that they most likely will continue into the future; trends so defined that it is possible to predict with a high degree of confidence what the agency business will be like over the next 10 years, if not longer into the future. These trends are continued overall growth; increased globalism; expansion in agency ability to offer diverse communication skills; continuing positive impact of media (technology) alternatives; and changes in the way agencies are compensated for their services.

Advertising flourishes in societies that are politically democratic, economically free, and where media alternatives are plentiful. The fact that the world appears to be moving more toward capitalism and away from socialism bodes well for advertising. According to Freedom House, as reported in the *New York Times* in October, 1988, more people in the world (38 percent) are living in free societies than ever in history. Even in the most antidemocratic societies, such as China and Russia, western-type activities are being encouraged.

This age of information transformation also bodes well for advertising. Advertising fundamentally functions to communicate information.

To the extent that countries are relaxing trade and media barriers—a la Europe in 1992—also bodes well for the agency business. The intention in Europe is to break down border restrictions between countries. This situation can only benefit advertising since there will be more homogeneity between countries and fewer restrictions regarding communication.

Advertising's growth will be global, meaning that the big global agencies will grow faster than their local counterparts. Local and regional agencies, accordingly, will look for international partners. The fundamental reason for these global agencies is that clients are moving toward internationalism. As clients become more global, their agencies must follow suit or lose business. Agencies that have global systems in place will benefit enormously.

Just as agencies must meet their clients' needs geographically, so must they meet them in terms of diversified services, such as direct marketing and sales promotion. A later part of this chapter discusses the barriers to successful integration of these agency services. Despite these barriers, clients increasingly are seeking a better integration of all the communication disciplines available within the marketing mix. Therefore, agencies will either have to create and develop these varied disciplines on their own or acquire them. Again, those agencies, such as Young & Rubicam and Ogilvy, that already have an array of disciplines, are ahead of the competition and in a position to grow at an accelerated rate.

Throughout the entire history of the advertising business, there has been a basic need for agencies to provide clients with business-building ideas. This basic need, however, has always existed in the context of a constantly changing world of media alternatives. All media, whether created to inform and/or entertain consumers, sooner or later accept advertising messages since advertising reduces the cost of the media to the customer. As new media, such as cable TV, are added, the original media still provide alternatives. Newspapers were supplemented by magazines, followed by radio, TV, cable TV, telemarketing, movies, and satellites. With each addition, the earlier media survived, adding greater variety to the mix available to the advertiser. In fact, radio is stronger today than before TV. The net result of all this technological change is that advertisers can be more selective, effective, and efficient than ever in reaching customers. This is definitely a positive development for the advertising business.

Methods of compensation, the ways in which clients pay agencies, also have changed over time. Today, an enormous range of compensation schemes exist. Within a given agency there may be as many compensation systems as there are clients. Compensation alternatives are discussed in Chapter 9, with a proposed "ideal" system. Suffice it to say that each advertiser should establish a fair and results-oriented compensation program to meet his or her unique needs. Not only should the agency make a decent profit, but it should also be possible for the agency to make greater profits based on the achievement of specified agreed-to goals. One thing appears certain; the tendency of clients to more or less unilaterally reduce agency compensation has had a detrimental effect upon agency performance, if not agency profit levels. As noted earlier in this book, faced with reduced compensation, an agency will try to maintain profit margins by the only means available to it—reduced service, either in quantity or quality. Therefore, clients who arbitrarily reduce agency compensation are doing themselves, as well as the whole advertising industry, a disservice. One good idea from an agency can make an enormous difference to a client's business. The smartest clients will recognize this and will develop compensation systems that not only allow the agency to service them profitably, but also will provide upside incentives. A true client-agency partnership can only come about if the compensation system is fair and equitable.

With all these positive trends, it is fair to say that the agency business, for all of its problems, will continue to grow and will therefore continue to be an exciting and rewarding profession for those who choose it.

THE FUTURE OF AGENCY INTEGRATED SERVICES

Clients, to one degree or another and for a period of at least 25 years, have expressed a desire for integrated marketing, meaning that two or more communication services (e.g., direct marketing, sales promotion, design, event marketing, public relations) would work in concert with advertising toward a common marketing objective. Agencies have recognized this desire and at the same time, have observed the financial success of these individual communication services. In many cases, agencies have acquired such services. Yet, except in rare circumstances, this mutually sought integration has not occurred.

Ironically, one major barrier to this integration has been and largely continues to be the inability of the clients' organizations to manage these agency services. If clients are organized in such a fashion that each element of their communication programs is resourced by a different part of their organizations, how can they expect their communication to be integrated?

A second barrier to effectively integrating agency services is agency separation of these services either by name or physically. Both methods of separation tend to work against offering clients a truly integrated communication program. By not giving the same name to the individual communication service as the parent company, the agency gives off signals that the individual service is something separate from the mainstream. This has a psychological effect that hinders true integration. The primary reason for a different name is that the individual communication service, which is usually an acquisition, has the name of its founder on the door. Agencies are reluctant to change a name, particularly if the founder continues to operate on a day-to-day basis. Nevertheless, integration is more successful if the individual horizontal communication services have the same name as the parent company.

Physical separation also retards integration. It does not help to develop an integrated communication program for a client if the individual services are blocks or cities apart from the mainstream agency. For obvious reasons, no agency would consider putting its account management and creative departments in separate buildings. The same logic applies to achieving integrated communication programs. The agency must provide for the physical proximity of these services if it wants them to work together effectively.

Perhaps the biggest barrier to integrated agency communication is the absence of a unified client compensation program for individual agency services. It stands to reason that agencies will attempt to sell those services that are most profitable, often when other services may be the very ones the client needs to solve a particular marketing problem. The dilemma rises particularly when the mainstream agency is working on some sort of a commission basis and the other individual service or services it is providing are on a fee-based compensation system. Here, the point clearly is that the compensation system should not get in the way of agency objectivity in providing the best all-around communication effort for its client. Therefore, clients must develop compensation plans that provide incentives for the total agency effort—plans that do not provide greater incentives for any individual agency sectors.

Related to this discussion is the absence of qualified total communication counselors at most agencies. Most agency account management individuals, regardless of the base discipline in which they are trained—direct marketing, sales promotion, or consumer advertising—are limited in their knowledge of the other horizontal disciplines. If a client asks an agency to solve a marketing problem, working from scratch and using any combination of agency services that makes sense, then the agency will need senior managers who are schooled and familiar with all of the service disciplines and who can make intelligent recommendations to the client.

In summary, assuming clients are desirous of marketing integration and total communication programs from their agencies and assuming that these same clients are organized in such a fashion as to manage such an agency process, then agencies must do the following in order to succeed in such efforts: they should name these individual services in common with the mainstream agency's name; they should physically integrate the services into the mainstream headquarters; and they should, while perhaps maintaining profit centers for the individual parts, negotiate with their clients to achieve a unified compensation program so that compensation does not hinder objective advice. Finally, agencies must train senior managers to be truly informed of the workings and benefits of the many individual services available so that these managers are capable of making the best judgments possible for clients seeking integration of agency resources. Until these barriers are dealt with and removed, truly integrated advertising agency communication programs will remain an elusive ideal.

INDEX